THE MAGIC

of

TINNED
FISH

CONTROL DE
CALIDAD
47

THE MAGIC
of
TINNED
FISH

Elevate Your Cooking with Canned Anchovies, Sardines, Mackerel, Crab, and Other Amazing Seafood

Chris McDade

Photographs by Dana Gallagher
Illustrations by Ali Elly

Artisan Books | New York

Library of Congress Cataloging-in-Publication Data

Names: McDade, Chris, author.
Title: The magic of tinned fish / Chris McDade.
Description: New York : Artisan, a division of Workman Publishing Co., Inc. [2021] | Includes index.
Identifiers: LCCN 2020042942 | ISBN 9781579659370 (hardcover)
Subjects: LCSH: Cooking (Fish) | Cooking (Seafood) | Canned fish. | Cooking (Canned foods) | LCGFT: Cookbooks.
Classification: LCC TX747 .M374 2021 | DDC 641.6/92—dc23
LC record available at https://lccn.loc.gov/2020042942

Design by Raphael Geroni
Food styling by Frances Boswell

Artisan books are available at special discounts when purchased in bulk for premiums and sales promotions as well as for fund-raising or educational use. Special editions or book excerpts also can be created to specification. For details, contact the Special Sales Director at the address below, or send an e-mail to specialmarkets@workman.com.

For speaking engagements, contact speakersbureau@workman.com.

Published by Artisan
A division of Workman Publishing Co., Inc.
225 Varick Street
New York, NY 10014-4381
artisanbooks.com

Artisan is a registered trademark of Workman Publishing Co., Inc.

Published simultaneously in Canada by Thomas Allen & Son, Limited

Printed in China

First printing, May 2021

10 9 8 7 6 5 4 3 2 1

To my beautiful wife, Natalie, and our little anchovy, Gus

A LA ANTIGUA
en aceite de oliva

matiz
ESPAÑA

Hand-Packed in
Galicia, Spain

PULPO
OCTOPUS
IN SPANISH OLIVE OIL

NET WT: 111g (4 oz)

EST. Roland 1934
SARDINAS

PESCA SALVAJE

— en —
ACEITE
DE OLIVA

PESO NETO 4.4 OZ. (125g)

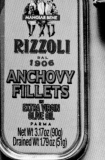

MANGIAR BENE

RIZZOLI
DAL
1906
ANCHOVY
FILLETS
EN
EXTRA VIRGIN
OLIVE OIL
PARMA
Net Wt 3.17oz (90g)
Drained Wt 1.79 oz (51g)

NET WEIGHT: 4 OZ (111g)
DRAINED WEIGHT: 2.4 OZ (69g)

made in
Galicia

Mussels
in PICKLED SAUCE

CABO
de PENAS
GRAN SELECCION

SARDINHAS
PORTUGUESAS EM AZEITE DE OLIVEIRA
E PIMENTO VERDE
PRODUTO DE PORTUGAL

Lucas
Brand

LUCAS & Cª Lª

NW 120g
(4.2 OZ)

Beach Cliff®
SARDINES

IN LOUISIANA
HOT SAUCE

NET WT 3.75 oz (106 g)   www.beachcliff.info

WILD
CAUGHT

Roland
FILLETS

patagonia
PROVISIONS

NET WT 4.2 OZ (120g)

LEMON CAPER
MACKEREL
in olive oil

LOT:L144P BEST BY: MAY 2023

Pescador
BRAND

SARDINHAS
EM TOMATE

LULAS
RECHEADAS
EM MOLHO
MEDITERRÂNICO

Lucas
Brand
SINCE 19..

LUCAS & Cª Lª

NET WT
115g (4..06z)

cole's
calamari

stuffed calamari
with rice, onion, tomato & spices

SUSTAINABLE
SELECTIONS

Net Wt 4.2 oz (120g)
bpa-free – no preservatives – gluten free

MACKEREL FILLETS IN OLIVE OIL
NET WT: 125 G (4 OZ)

Cavala Portuguesa
em azeite

Peso líq: 120g

DA MOR
GA GA
DA

BOM
PETISCO
SARDINHAS
em azeite

VitalChoice
Wild Sardine
in Extra-Virgin Olive Oil
Net Wt. 4.4 oz (125g)

SARDINES IN TOMATO SAUCE
SARDINES À LA SAUCE TOMATE

PORTHOS

NET WT.
4.4 oz
125 g

SINCE 1917

CONTENTS

INTRODUCTION

FISH AND SHELLFISH HAVE LONG BEEN CONSIDERED DELICIOUS when served fresh. Just-caught fish cooked over coals or simply panfried with only a squeeze of lemon juice is undoubtedly satisfying, but what do you do when fresh fish is out of season or not available where you live? Like fruits and vegetables, seafood has a terroir and a time when each fish is at its best. This is where tinned fish come in. The best brands of tinned seafood are processed shortly after being caught, using only the finest quality fish. Thanks to a commitment to quality by the fishermen and canneries, quick, affordable, and nutrient-dense meals can be available any time of year, anywhere, and are only a tin away.

Generally considered to be an economical snack food, tinned fish can actually serve as the focal point of many elevated dishes and of any meal. The recipes in this book prove that tinned fish can be just as, if not more, versatile and delicious than their fresh counterparts. From a smoked oyster on a cracker to a delicious anchovy sauce poured over a charred steak, tinned fish pack a lot of flavor and will help you become a better and more confident cook.

My love for preserved anchovies is well documented by people who know me or have eaten at my restaurant, Popina, in Brooklyn, New York. The little fish that pack an umami punch bring so much flavor to my cooking, both at home and at the restaurant. While I always enjoy anchovies straight from the tin, they are often a hidden ingredient in my sauces and dressings; they give the dishes I cook more complexity.

As my love for anchovies continues to grow, I have found myself wondering what other joys hide behind the colorful boxes and pull tabs of the tinned fish culture, and it has led me to cook with all kinds of tinned seafood and shellfish—from mackerel to octopus. What I now understand is that the tinned fish market is as diverse as it is delicious, and for good reason.

Tinned seafood is convenient, healthful, and honest; there's no hiding the quality when there are only one or two ingredients in the can. Tinned fish is simplicity at its best. There is something pretty phenomenal about being able to carry half of your daily protein requirement in the pocket of your jeans—and for the same price as a trip to the nearest fast-food restaurant! In Portugal, where tinned fish is eaten regularly, it *is* a version of fast food. Although a burger and fries might appear to be delicious and filling, they're merely hiding behind a processed curtain of salt and fat. Tinned fish, on the other hand, are a far better choice; they're packed with vitamins and nutrients, and they are also a sustainable option. Tinned fish require no refrigeration, thus saving energy during storage. Lastly, because of the small serving sizes and the fact that they do not start to spoil until opened, tinned fish involve minimal food waste as well.

A LITTLE BIT OF HISTORY

Like many of the greatest inventions of all time, tinned food was born in response to a wartime problem. This one was feeding the troops. In 1795, the French army offered a prize of 12,000 francs (250,000 US dollars today) to anyone who could safely find a way to store food so that it could travel with the soldiers on the front lines without spoiling. In 1810, French chef Nicolas Appert devised a way of boiling foods and sealing them in glass bottles. The first "canned" food was born, and Appert claimed his prize.

Shortly after Appert's achievement, a British shop owner by the name of Peter Durand got the first patent for a tin container. By 1820, Durand was supplying the entire Royal Navy with safe preserved foods. A Breton man who had been closely following the work of Appert and Durand was inspired by the tinning of foods and became the first person to put sardines into tins. This man's name was Pierre-Joseph Colin, and his single factory in Brittany quickly expanded to three in order to supply most of the French soldiers with their protein needs for the duration of the Napoleonic Wars. Before the tin, preserved seafood was historically pickled or salted to get it inland without refrigeration.

In 1840, a French sailboat carrying a supply of tinned sardines crashed off the coast of Spain. Exploring the wreckage, the Spaniards discovered the French

TIN (CAN) VS. GLASS

Most tinned fish come in just that: tins (or cans). But some fish, such as ancho-vies, can also be purchased preserved in glass jars. Glass jars are good because they allow you to get a glimpse of what's inside, the glass won't impart any flavor to the product itself and is resistant to salt and acid, and the jars can be easily recycled. However, the light exposure with food stored in glass jars is almost never good (it allows the food to spoil sooner), and the jars are often heavier and more fragile than their tinned counterparts.

Tins are not as fragile as glass, so they are much easier for the producer to use. In addition, the products to be stored in tins can be cooled immediately, and the tins take up less space (making them easier to transport), can take quite a beating and still maintain their integrity, and are completely recyclable (in fact, a tin can is generally recycled and reused without any loss in quality). However, tins can be tricky to open if not fitted with a pull top. But a can opener should do the trick, and you shouldn't have to rely on a bayonet like soldiers once did to eat their dinners.

invention, and the rest, as they say, is history. The Spanish began tinning sardines and many types of shellfish, including cockles and mussels. This technique quickly made its way to Lisbon, Portugal, which remains a working fishing port to this day. Sardines account for nearly one-third of the total yearly seafood catch for Portugal. This explains why tinned sardines have become so popular there. The local sardines are not only nutritious and flavorful but also inexpensive because of their abundance.

For many years in America, tinned fish was largely viewed as food for the poor. There are several factors that led to this perception. Tinned fish do not smell like fresh fish and are generally served at room temperature. Americans were used to their seafood smelling fresh and being stored cold. Also, if you didn't live close to the coast, traditionally you didn't eat fish because refrigerated trucks for transport and proper storage methods hadn't yet been invented. From the late 1800s through the early 1900s, many Europeans made their way to the United States. They emigrated for a better life and did their best to conform to the new society. That meant that meat was the prized food for these immigrants, and the cheap tinned fish of their homelands was a relic and a not-fond remembrance of their previous lives.

Today, thankfully, tinned fish is having its moment. Why? People all over the globe are starting to understand that fish in a tin is delicious and deserving of a place on restaurant menus as well as in their cupboard at home. It's full of nutrients, sustainable, and packed with flavor, making us change the way we think about seafood.

COOKING FROM THE BOOK

The recipes in this book are rooted in the food traditions of Italy, Spain, France, and the United States, primarily, but with modern upgrades. They'll teach you to use tinned fish in ways you never realized possible. Whether in a simple dip made with smoked oysters or an elaborate lamb roast studded with anchovies, the versatility of tinned fish will surprise and delight you. It can be highlighted as the main ingredient in a dish, but just as often, the fish plays a supporting role, such as in an herbaceous salsa verde or flaked into a hearty bowl of chowder.

Few things are as frustrating as reading through a recipe only to be discouraged by an ingredients list full of items that are difficult to track down. So with that in mind, the ingredients on these pages should be easy to find at your local grocer. And when you're faced with making a choice on which tin to pick up, refer to The Best Tinned Fish (following page) for a list of my favorites.

When you keep tinned fish on hand, you can feed yourself affordably, sustainably, and deliciously. My hope is that you'll turn to this book again and again to nourish yourself with a variety of hearty and healthful fish. Happy cooking.

WHAT TO LOOK FOR

Often caught, cleaned, and tinned during their peak season, the seafood that you buy in a tin is by and large first-class, with a delicate texture and refined flavor. When searching for quality tinned fish, follow these three simple rules.

1. Stay away from anything too cheap! Although you are dealing with fish in a tin, it's still fish. You wouldn't look for discounted fresh fish at the grocery store, so don't do that here. Anything under four dollars a tin is probably not of good quality.

2. Tinned fish is often stored in oil or water. Skip the water-packed options completely and choose brands that use quality olive oil and marinades. Though it's true that water-packed fish retain more of their omega-3s, the flavor of fish stored in good oil is just so much better.

3. Know where your food comes from. You should be curious about the origin of anything you consume, and tinned fish should be no different. As a general rule, look at the catch method (hook and line, pole trawl, pot caught), where the fish was caught (different waters have healthier populations of certain species than others), and the species (dishonest canneries sometimes fill cans with a cheaper variety than the one represented on the can). If you're not well versed in these terms, simply ask someone at your specialty food store or read information online at SeafoodWatch.org for the most sustainable choices. Also, don't be fooled by tricky names and lack of information on the tins. When in doubt, don't buy it!

THE BEST TINNED FISH

The world of tinned seafood can be a bit intimidating if you don't know what you're looking for. To make it easier for you, here is a list of my favorites. These are all brands you can trust.

- AGROMAR *(Asturias, Spain).* Anchovies and sea urchin fresh from the cool waters of the Atlantic Ocean.

- CABO DE PEÑAS *(Galicia, Spain).* Plump, tender, and intense sardines.

- COLE'S *(Maine, USA).* Wonderful smoked trout and mackerel farmed, fished, and canned in fishing towns around the globe.

- DON BOCARTE *(Cantabria, Spain).* Especially the anchovies. A bit pricey but totally worth it.

- EKONE OYSTER CO *(Washington, USA).* Delicious oysters from Willapa Bay via a small, family-run operation.

- J.M. CLAYTON COMPANY *(Maryland, USA).* Blue crabmeat straight out of the Chesapeake Bay, processed without any chemicals or preservatives.

- JOSÉ GOURMET *(Lisbon, Portugal).* First-class sardines, smoked trout, and mackerel harvested from the best waters in and around Portugal.

- LA BRUJULA *(Galicia, Spain).* Delicious squid and clams that are hand cleaned by local women.

- MATIZ *(Galicia, Spain).* Sardines and shellfish harvested in the traditional way, respecting the biological cycles of the species and without harming other sea life.

- ORTIZ *(Bilbao, Spain).* Great anchovies from a legendary producer; it's an easy brand to find and a relatively inexpensive one, too.

- POLLASTRINI DI ANZIO *(Rome, Italy).* Wild-caught and locally inexpensive sardines and mackerel that provide incredible quality for the money.

- RAMÓN PEÑA *(Galicia, Spain).* Sustainable Galician seafood from a purveyor that has been around for more than ninety years; their mussels and octopus are especially good.

For a list of where to buy tinned fish online, see Resources, page 196.

ANCHOVIES

ENGRAULIDAE

ANCHOVIES ARE ONE OF THE ANCHORS OF THE OCEAN'S food chain, providing most of your favorite fish, such as halibut and salmon, with their own nutrient-dense meals. For us, the anchovy is a delicious and humble ingredient that packs a real punch when you consider its size and price tag. The recipes in this chapter will teach you all the ways anchovies can add an extra dimension to your cooking—ways that will keep you reaching for their little tins over and over.

Anchovies have played an important role in kitchens and cultures all over the world for centuries. Originating in Greece and championed by the Romans, garum, a fermented fish sauce, was one of the earliest uses of anchovies. It was used to season meats, vegetables, and even some desserts. The Romans were so fond of garum that major trade routes were created to get the elixir from other parts of Europe to the Eternal City. The best-quality sauce could fetch prices similar to those of the best perfumes.

Anchovies thrive in the cool, brackish waters of the Mediterranean. Not surprisingly, they are widely used in Italy, Spain, and France, as well as in Portugal and Asia. People in these cultures eat anchovies fresh, salted, dried, brined, and fermented into sauces. Anchovies are responsible for Venice's pasta with anchovies and onions; Spain's most famous pintxo, the Gilda; France's pissaladière; and countless other classic recipes.

Not only are anchovies versatile and delicious, they are also extremely good for you. They are an impressive source of omega-3 fatty acids, the stuff that promotes a healthy heart and even helps battle depression. Anchovies are also a wonderful source of calcium, magnesium, niacin, phosphorus, and protein. The positive effects of eating anchovies are well documented—it helps promote strong bones, repair tissue and cells, and minimize the risk of cardiovascular disease, and can aid in weight loss.

If those aren't enough reasons to pop a tin of anchovies and get cooking, how about the fact that anchovies deliver that fifth taste in food, umami. Ever wonder why a chef's food tastes so good? It's umami, which is often associated with mushrooms, miso, Parmesan cheese, and meats. Anchovies help you sneak some umami flavor into whatever you're cooking, whether it's pasta with anchovies and onions (see page 39) or a cast-iron steak with anchovy butter (see page 45).

WHAT'S IN THE TIN

You generally see anchovies preserved three ways: in vinegar, in oil, or in salt.

Anchovies preserved in vinegar are a Spanish classic and an excellent way to add a zingy bite to your favorite salad. Vinegar-marinated anchovies, called boquerones, do not come packed in tins but rather on plastic trays sealed with plastic film. They are usually eaten with a roasted pepper or slice of bread at bars across Spain.

Then there are anchovies stored in oil and those packed in salt. Essentially there is no difference between these two products. Anchovies stored in oil start as salt-packed anchovies that then get rinsed of salt, cleaned, and given a bath of olive oil to rest in. Anchovies packed in salt are generally sold in larger tins because they have a much longer shelf life than their oil-stored counterparts. Anchovies stored in oil can also come in large tins but can be found in 2-ounce (55 g) tins in most markets. These smaller tins usually hold eight to ten anchovy fillets. For the recipes in this book, you can use anchovies packed in oil or salt. But when using salt-packed, you need to clean them (see How to Clean Salted Anchovies, on the following pages), so you'll be saving yourself some extra work if you use those stored in olive oil.

HOW TO CLEAN SALTED ANCHOVIES

If you are using anchovies packed in salt, you must first clean them before continuing with the recipes. Follow these steps.

1. Carefully remove the anchovies from the tin and place them on a clean plate. Discard the salt and recycle the tin.

2. One by one, rinse each fish under cold, gently running water.

3. Place on paper towels to dry. Some anchovies are cured less than others. If the anchovies are soft but plump, you can skip the next two steps.

4. Fill a large bowl with cold water and soak the fish until they begin to soften, about 15 minutes.

5. Once the anchovies are soft, remove them from the water and transfer them to a paper towel.

6. For each fish, starting from the tail end, carefully pull the top fillet toward the head until it is removed.

7. With a firm hold on the tail of the remaining fillet, pull the spine toward the head until it releases. Discard the spine.

8. Pull away and discard the silver skin, viscera, and anything else that doesn't look like flesh.

9. Dry the fillets with paper towels again and transfer to an airtight container, such as a lidded glass jar, filled with enough olive oil to cover the cleaned fillets. The anchovies are now ready to use. The cleaned fillets packed in oil will keep for at least 1 month.

ANCHOVIES, BREAD, AND BUTTER

At first glance, there isn't much to a piece of bread smeared with a little butter and topped with a few anchovies; but after the initial bite, you'll understand the wonder of anchovies. It would be silly to call this a recipe. Making this snack is more of a lesson in contrasting flavors and textures between the fatty and smooth butter, the salty anchovy, and the warm, crunchy bread. Anchovies on toast is delicious year-round, but it makes an amazing light lunch when paired with a salad during the long hot days of summer. This straightforward combination is perfect on its own, but feel free to add sliced radish or soft-boiled eggs. Reach for a glass of txakoli or other crisp white wine to drink alongside.

SERVES 1

Your favorite unsalted butter, at room temperature (not too hard, not too soft)

Crusty bread, slightly toasted

A tin of the best anchovies you can find

A bit of lemon zest

Spread a generous amount of butter on the toasted bread. Lay the anchovies atop the butter and finish with a couple pinches of lemon zest. Take a bite and enjoy!

PISSALADIÈRE

A traditional food of the South of France, pissaladière is a flatbread topped with caramelized onions, black olives, and anchovies. The crust is typically a thick pizza dough of sorts, but here the recipe is simplified by using premade puff pastry. Cooking the onions low and slow is important; you need their sweetness to balance the saltiness of the anchovies. Pissaladière can be served hot or at room temperature.

SERVES 6

2 tablespoons unsalted butter

2 tablespoons olive oil

8 cups (680 g) thinly sliced yellow onions

18 anchovy fillets

4 sprigs thyme

2 sprigs rosemary

¼ cup (60 ml) red wine

1 tablespoon red wine vinegar

Kosher salt and freshly ground black pepper

One 14-ounce (395 g) sheet frozen puff pastry, thawed for 2 to 3 hours

½ cup (65 g) pitted Niçoise olives

½ cup (75 g) sliced oil-packed sun-dried tomatoes

In a large skillet or Dutch oven, heat the butter and olive oil over medium heat. Once the butter has melted, add the onions and stir to coat. Add the anchovies, thyme, and rosemary. Cook until the onions are soft, sweet, and a lovely tanned color. This will take around 1 hour, but make sure you stir every 5 minutes or so and more frequently when the onions are close to being finished.

About 5 minutes before the onion/anchovy mixture is ready, add the wine and vinegar to deglaze the pan. Take care to scrape the bottom of the pan using a wooden spoon or silicone spatula. Season with salt and pepper. Cook for another 5 minutes before transferring to a plate to cool.

Position a rack in the lowest slot of the oven and preheat the oven to 425°F (220°C).

Press the puff pastry onto a 12 × 18-inch (30 × 45 cm) sheet pan. Leave a little overhang around the edges. Evenly spread the caramelized onions onto the puff pastry. Evenly scatter the olives across the onions, followed by the sun-dried tomatoes.

Bake until the bottom of the tart is golden and crisp, about 25 minutes. If you're not sure if the bottom is cooked, use a heatproof spatula to gently lift an edge of the tart. Cut the tart into 6 squares and enjoy right away or save for later in the day.

GRILLED BROCCOLI WITH ANCHOVIES, PISTACHIOS, AND GREEN GODDESS DRESSING

A California classic, Green Goddess is a tangy, herby buttermilk dressing. It pairs well with broccoli, which becomes wonderfully charred and tender after just a few minutes on the grill. The addition of anchovies here is a perfect example of how their umami quality rounds out a dressing without becoming the dominant flavor.

SERVES 2 AS AN ENTRÉE OR 4 AS AN APPETIZER

GREEN GODDESS DRESSING

¾ cup (170 g) mayonnaise

2 tablespoons sour cream

1 teaspoon yellow mustard

2 tablespoons minced fresh parsley

1 tablespoon minced fresh mint

1 tablespoon minced fresh tarragon

1 tablespoon minced fresh chives

1 tablespoon minced jalapeño

4 anchovy fillets, minced

3 tablespoons buttermilk

2 teaspoons olive oil

Lemon, for squeezing

GRILLED BROCCOLI AND HERBS

2 medium stalks broccoli, stems trimmed off, cut into large florets

3 tablespoons olive oil

1 teaspoon kosher salt

Freshly ground black pepper

5 anchovy fillets

2 tablespoons fresh mint

2 tablespoons fresh tarragon

2 tablespoons fresh parsley

2 tablespoons chopped pistachios

To make the Green Goddess dressing: In a food processor, combine the mayonnaise, sour cream, mustard, chopped herbs, jalapeño, and anchovies and pulse until the ingredients are well incorporated. (It's important to mince the herbs before putting them in the food processor, so that you don't end up with bruised and stringy bits of herbs in the final product.) With the food processor running, slowly drizzle in the buttermilk. Follow with the olive oil and finish with a squeeze of lemon juice.

If using the dressing right away, leave it in the food processor to save yourself the extra dirty bowl. If saving the dressing for later, transfer it to an airtight container and store for up to 3 days.

Continued

To make the broccoli: Heat a grill to medium-high. (Alternatively, heat a grill pan over medium-high heat.)

In a large bowl, gently massage the broccoli florets with the olive oil, salt, and pepper to taste.

Place the broccoli on the grill and set the bowl to the side. Cook the broccoli, turning the pieces every 2 minutes or so, until they are nicely charred and tender, about 8 minutes.

Return the broccoli to the bowl and toss with as much or as little Green Goddess dressing as you'd like.

Arrange the dressed broccoli on a serving platter and scatter the anchovy fillets over the top, followed by the herbs and finally the chopped pistachios, before diving in.

ANCHOVY, PARSLEY, AND PECORINO SANDWICH

This sandwich is simple, quick to make, and full of flavor. It's also a great base for your favorite market vegetables. Fill it with fresh tomatoes in the summer, roasted squash in the fall, sautéed kale in the winter, and raw fennel in the spring . . . the possibilities are endless.

=== MAKES 1 SANDWICH ===

3 tablespoons olive oil

⅓ cup (10 g) finely chopped fresh parsley

4 anchovy fillets, roughly chopped

1 clove garlic, finely chopped

Grated zest and juice of ¼ lemon

1 ciabatta sandwich roll, split

1 ounce (30 g) Pecorino Toscano or other young sheep's-milk cheese, thinly sliced

Fresh or roasted vegetables (optional)

In a small bowl, combine 2 tablespoons of the olive oil, the parsley, anchovies, garlic, lemon zest, and lemon juice and stir to combine. What you are left with is a chunky and pungent salsa with just enough oil to help carry the flavors on the bread.

Spread half of the parsley mixture on the top side of a split ciabatta roll and spread the remaining half on the bottom. Cover the bottom piece of the roll with the sliced pecorino. (If you want to add roasted vegetables to your sandwich, place half of the cheese down first, then the vegetables, then the rest of the cheese.)

In a nonstick skillet, heat the remaining 1 tablespoon olive oil over medium-high heat. Place the sandwich in the pan top side down and cook for 2 minutes. Flip the sandwich and cook for another 2 minutes. Eat the sandwich while it is warm.

MARKET VEGETABLES
WITH BAGNA CAUDA

Every fall in Italy's Piedmont region, there is a celebration of the year's grape harvest that includes friends drinking some of the world's great red wines and sharing bubbling bowls of bagna cauda with seasonal vegetables for dipping. Some purists will tell you that only peppers and cardoons should be served alongside the "hot bath" of anchovies and garlic, while others, including me, will have any raw or cooked vegetable with this delicious dip. Bagna cauda also makes a wonderful salad dressing and is great drizzled over your morning eggs.

SERVES 4 AS AN APPETIZER

15 cloves garlic

½ cup (120 ml) olive oil

14 anchovy fillets

8 tablespoons (115 g) unsalted butter

Fresh vegetables, such as peppers, cauliflower, endive, and fennel, cut into 1-bite pieces

Hard-boiled eggs, cut in half, for serving

Crusty bread, for serving

Peel the garlic cloves. Mince half and thinly slice the other half.

In a small saucepan, combine the olive oil, all the garlic, and the anchovies and cook over low heat until the garlic is soft and fills your kitchen with its intoxicating aroma, about 20 minutes. Take care not to let the garlic brown, by stirring every few minutes.

Slowly stir in the butter before bringing to an aggressive simmer over medium heat.

Carefully pour into a small bowl and serve alongside fresh market vegetables, hard-boiled eggs, and bread.

ROASTED ROMAINE AND MUSHROOMS WITH CAESAR DRESSING

Creamy, lemony, and perfectly punched with anchovies, Caesar dressing is a classic for good reason. Here it pairs wonderfully with umami-rich roasted mushrooms and charred romaine lettuce. You could also try the dressing as a dip for raw cucumbers or on top of toast with roasted Brussels sprouts.

SERVES 2

CAESAR DRESSING

6 anchovy fillets, chopped

1 large clove garlic, chopped

2 tablespoons fresh lemon juice

1 teaspoon Worcestershire sauce

1 teaspoon Dijon mustard

2 tablespoons grated Parmesan cheese

2 egg yolks

1 teaspoon grapeseed or other neutral oil

2 tablespoons olive oil

Freshly ground black pepper

MUSHROOMS AND ROMAINE

1½ pounds (680 g) maitake mushrooms, trimmed and cut into small clusters

¼ cup plus 2 tablespoons (90 ml) olive oil

Kosher salt and freshly ground black pepper

2 large heads romaine lettuce, halved lengthwise, tough stem end removed

Lemon wedges, for serving (optional)

Preheat the oven to 425°F (220°C). Line a sheet pan with foil.

To make the Caesar dressing: In a food processor, combine the anchovies, garlic, lemon juice, Worcestershire sauce, and mustard. Pulse a few times to fully incorporate. Add the Parmesan and egg yolks and pulse a couple more times.

With the food processor running, slowly drizzle in the neutral oil, followed by the olive oil, until the dressing is fully emulsified. (If the dressing should separate on you, see the Note for how to rescue it.)

To prepare the mushrooms and romaine: Lay out the mushrooms in a single layer on the prepared sheet pan. Drizzle with ¼ cup (60 ml) of the olive oil and season liberally with salt and pepper. Gently toss to coat.

Transfer to the oven and roast until the mushrooms have tender hearts and golden, crispy petals, 30 to 35 minutes, tossing halfway through.

When the mushrooms are cooked, set aside, and place the romaine on the used sheet pan. Coat the romaine with the remaining 2 tablespoons olive oil and season with additional salt and pepper.

Turn the romaine cut side down and roast until the centers are soft and the tips are charred, about 10 minutes.

Place the romaine cut side up on your favorite plate or platter, drizzle with some Caesar dressing, top with the roasted mushrooms, and drizzle with more dressing. Serve with a few lemon wedges, if you'd like.

NOTE: If the dressing starts to separate, don't worry; it happens to everyone, and it's easy to fix. Transfer the broken dressing to a bowl and clean out the bowl of the food processor. Add 1 teaspoon of lemon juice to the food processor and add a small amount of the Caesar dressing. Pulse to emulsify. Gradually add the rest of the Caesar dressing while constantly pulsing until the consistency is creamy.

SPAGHETTI WITH PUTTANESCA SAUCE

Rumored to have been named in the mid-twentieth century for Neapolitan ladies of the night, this pungent and flavorful pasta takes less than 30 minutes to put together, making it a good choice for a weeknight meal. It's versatile, too: For a lighter and more herbaceous pasta, swap the black olives for green and add some chopped basil.

SERVES 2

5 tablespoons (75 ml) olive oil

2 cloves garlic, thinly sliced

5 anchovy fillets

2 tablespoons chopped black olives

2 tablespoons capers, chopped

1 cup (240 g) canned crushed tomatoes

¼ teaspoon chili flakes

¼ teaspoon dried oregano

Kosher salt

6 ounces (170 g) spaghetti or other pasta of your choice

2 tablespoons chopped fresh parsley

Bring a large pot of water to a boil over high heat for the pasta. This can take up to 20 minutes, depending on your stove. Use this time to gather the rest of your ingredients.

Starting with a cold skillet, gently heat 3 tablespoons of the olive oil along with the garlic over medium heat, taking care to soften the garlic but avoid browning it. Starting things in a cold pan like this allows you to have a bit more control over the doneness of the garlic while infusing maximum flavor into the oil. The idea here is to have soft garlic and fragrant oil. This should take only 1 to 2 minutes. This is when you really start to develop the punchy flavors that puttanesca is known for.

Add the anchovy fillets to the garlic oil and, using the back of a spoon to gently mash the fillets against the bottom of your pan, cook for 1 minute. No need to be aggressive here as the anchovies will break down on their own as well.

Add the olives and capers and cook for 1 minute. Again, the goal here is to extract the flavors into the oil and fill your kitchen with the wonderful perfume of the sauce.

Continued

Add the tomatoes, chili flakes, and oregano. Cook for 3 minutes, stirring, making sure the tomatoes don't stick to the bottom of the pan while the sauce thickens.

Add enough salt to the boiling water so that it reminds you of a less salty sea. Add the pasta and cook according to the package directions, stirring the pasta every 2 minutes or so to ensure that it doesn't stick together. Taste a noodle a minute or so before the end of the suggested cooking time to ensure that your pasta comes out al dente.

Just before it's time to remove the pasta from the boiling water, add ⅓ cup (80 ml) of the pasta water to the pan. Adding pasta water is a trick that not only helps to season the finished product but also utilizes the starch shed by the pasta to make the pasta sauce creamier in texture.

Increase the heat to medium-high and add the drained cooked pasta to the sauce. Cook, constantly stirring and tossing, until the sauce clings to the noodles and there is about ¼ cup (60 ml) left at the bottom of the pan, about 2 minutes.

Stir in the parsley, divide the pasta between two bowls, and serve.

PASTA WITH
ANCHOVIES AND ONIONS

Known in the home kitchens along Venetian canals simply as salsa, this ancient recipe comprises minimal ingredients found in most Italian home pantries. It is traditionally eaten on fasting or meatless days as a way to show sorrow for your sins, but it is now enjoyed year-round in osterias all over the region.

SERVES 2

¼ yellow onion

1 clove garlic, minced

3 tablespoons unsalted butter

1 tablespoon olive oil

Kosher salt

6 ounces (170 g) bucatini or other pasta of your choice

8 anchovy fillets

¼ cup (25 g) grated Parmesan cheese, plus more for serving

1 tablespoon chopped fresh parsley

1 tablespoon fresh lemon juice

Bring a large pot of water to a boil over high heat for the pasta. This can take up to 20 minutes, depending on your stove. While waiting on the water, very thinly slice the onion, trying your best to cut it into slices ⅛ inch (3 mm) thick. A bit thicker is okay, too.

Starting with a cold pan, gently heat the garlic, 1 tablespoon of the butter, and the olive oil over low heat until the garlic becomes fragrant, about 1 minute. Add the onion and increase the heat to medium. Make sure you give the pan a toss every other minute and take care not to brown the butter. Once the onions are soft, after about 12 minutes, reduce the heat to low.

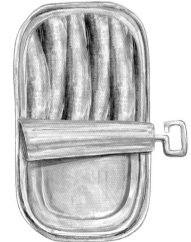

Add enough salt to the boiling water so that it reminds you of a less salty sea. Add the pasta and cook according to the package directions, stirring the pasta every

2 minutes or so to ensure that it doesn't stick together. Taste a noodle a minute or so before the end of the suggested cooking time to ensure that your pasta comes out al dente.

Just before it's time to remove the pasta from the boiling water, add ⅓ cup (80 ml) of the pasta water and the anchovies to the onion mixture and bring it to an aggressive simmer. Add the pasta and continue cooking, constantly stirring and flipping, until about 3 tablespoons of liquid remain in the pan. Stir in the remaining 2 tablespoons butter and remove from the heat. Add the Parmesan, parsley, and lemon juice and stir until fully incorporated.

Divide the pasta between two bowls and top with more Parmesan.

THE GILDA

The Gilda, the Basque Country's most famous pintxo, was created in 1946 in one of the many bars on the busy streets of San Sebastián. A pintxo is a small snack usually held together with a toothpick or a piece of bread, and pintxos have become ubiquitous in nightspots in the Basque region of Spain. Bold, spicy, and salty, the Gilda was named after Rita Hayworth's character in the movie of the same name. This simple pintxo relies heavily on the quality of its ingredients, especially the anchovy.

=========== MAKES 1 SMALL PINTXO ===========

1 guindilla pepper (pickled peppers sometimes sold as piparras)

1 Manzanilla olive, pitted

1 anchovy fillet

On a small skewer or toothpick, thread the pepper, then the anchovy, and finish with the olive. Pour yourself a cold glass of vermut and enjoy immediately.

CAST-IRON RIB-EYE STEAK
WITH ANCHOVY BUTTER

While this recipe suggests using a rib eye, there's really no cut of steak that won't work well with anchovy butter. Ask your trusted butcher for whatever looks the best in their case, and you'll be happy. While pairing anchovies and steak may seem a bit odd, the two are actually a perfect match. Anchovies are often hiding in your steak sauce anyway, so I'm positive this will become your go-to accompaniment when cooking your favorite cut of beef. Once you get the hang of making anchovy butter, you can use it other ways; it is equally delicious slathered on warm bread or thrown in a pan with pasta for a super-quick and simple meal.

SERVES 2

ANCHOVY BUTTER

2 sticks (230 g) unsalted butter, at room temperature

10 anchovy fillets, minced

4 cloves garlic, minced

Grated zest of 1 lemon

1 tablespoon fresh lemon juice

2 teaspoons ground toasted fennel seeds

STEAK

1¼-pound (565 g) rib-eye steak

1 tablespoon canola oil

Kosher salt and freshly ground black pepper

To make the anchovy butter: In a food processor, combine the butter, anchovies, garlic, lemon zest, lemon juice, and fennel seeds and pulse until all the ingredients are completely incorporated.

Use a silicone spatula to transfer the butter to a plastic container with a lid. Use the butter right away or store in the refrigerator for up to 2 weeks or freeze for up to 6 months.

To make the steak: Take the steak out of the fridge and let it sit on the counter for 30 minutes before you start cooking. This helps even the temperature of the meat, which makes it easier to cook to the desired doneness.

Heat a cast-iron skillet over high heat and pour in the canola oil.

Continued

Liberally season the steak with salt and pepper. Not only does this enhance the flavor of the meat, it creates a delicious crust. When the canola oil begins to smoke, add the rib eye to the pan. Cook it on each side for 4 to 5 minutes for medium-rare.

Transfer the steak to a platter and top with as much anchovy butter as you'd like. The heat of the steak will melt the better and create a delicious pool for resting. Allow to rest for 8 minutes, then slice, spoon some of the melted butter over the rib eye, and serve.

HAM-STUFFED TROUT
WITH SALSA VERDE

Salsa verde literally translates to "green sauce," and it is just that: a tangy and bright sauce—not dissimilar from chimichurri—that pairs well with everything from the trout and ham in this recipe to roasted chicken. It can even be spooned over your scrambled eggs. So make sure to keep any leftover salsa to enjoy later; it'll keep in the fridge in a lidded container for up to a week.

SERVES 2

SALSA VERDE

1 cup (30 g) flat-leaf parsley, finely chopped

2 tablespoons fresh marjoram or oregano, finely chopped

½ jalapeño, seeded and finely chopped

1½ tablespoons capers, finely chopped

4 anchovy fillets, finely chopped

2 cloves garlic, finely chopped

½ cup (120 ml) olive oil

1½ teaspoons Dijon mustard

Grated zest of ½ lemon

TROUT

2 whole trout (about 8 ounces/225 g each), butterflied and pin bones removed

Kosher salt and freshly ground black pepper

3 slices country ham, serrano ham, or prosciutto

1 tablespoon olive oil

Lemon wedges, for serving

To make the salsa verde: In a small bowl, mix together the parsley, marjoram, jalapeño, capers, anchovies, garlic, olive oil, mustard, and lemon zest and give everything a gentle but thorough stir with a fork. You want to make sure the mixture is a harmonious blend of the ingredients.

To prepare the trout: Lightly rinse the skin of the trout under a little running water and pat dry well with paper towels. Season the flesh with salt and pepper (you will season the skin right before cooking) and place 1 slice of ham in each fish. Close the fish and set aside on a plate.

In a pan large enough to fit both trout side by side, heat the olive oil over medium-high heat until it starts to shimmer. Add the remaining slice of ham and cook until it starts to become crispy, about 5 minutes. You'll want to flip the slice of ham once or twice to ensure maximum crispiness.

Remove the ham from the pan and drain on a paper towel.

Season both sides of the trout with salt and pepper and immediately add both fish to the pan now containing the olive oil and ham fat. Cook the fish over medium heat or until the skin is crispy and the fillets are fully cooked, 5 to 6 minutes per side. Transfer to a plate lined with paper towels.

To serve, place each trout in the center of a plate. Spoon over as much or as little salsa verde as you'd like. Break half of the crispy ham over each plate, add a lemon wedge, and you're good to go!

ROASTED LAMB WITH ANCHOVIES, ROSEMARY, AND POTATOES

Lamb and anchovies are a truly perfect pairing. Here the little fish go a long way in bringing out the best parts of a lamb; they get stuffed inside the meat to permeate the entire roast. Anchovies give the lamb incredible savoriness without any fishy flavor. Think of this recipe when you have to feed a crowd or you have a few hungry diners at your table.

SERVES 6 TO 8

4½ pounds (2 kg) bone-in leg of lamb (ask your butcher to trim it for you)

2 cloves garlic, peeled

Kosher salt and freshly ground black pepper

Large handful of rosemary sprigs, leaves picked from half and minced

Two 2-ounce (55 g) tins anchovy fillets with the oil

¾ cup (175 ml) white wine

1 pound (455 g) Yukon Gold potatoes, cut into ½-inch-thick (1.5 cm) rounds

Remove the lamb from the refrigerator about 1 hour before you're ready to start cooking. Preheat the oven to 350°F (180°C).

Place the garlic, a large pinch or two of salt, and a few cracks of pepper in a mortar. Use the pestle to break down the garlic, then add the minced rosemary and one tin of anchovies, including the oil. Continue mashing until it becomes a smooth paste. (Alternatively, you can mince everything with your knife and mix it together in a small bowl.) Set aside.

Place the lamb in a large roasting pan. Using a paring knife, make ten 1-inch (2.5 cm) slits in the lamb. Stuff each hole with a small spoonful of the paste, along with 1 anchovy fillet and a sprig of rosemary. Pour the remaining paste and any anchovy oil over the lamb. Confidently massage it into the flesh.

Pour half of the wine over the lamb and allow it to drip into the roasting pan. Cover the pan loosely with foil and transfer to the oven.

Continued

Roast the lamb for 30 minutes. Remove the pan from the oven and remove the foil (save the foil for later). Leave the oven on and increase the temperature to 400°F (200°C).

Using a large spoon, spoon the roasting juices over the lamb, taking care that every piece of the leg gets a little love. Quickly transfer the lamb from the pan to a large sheet of foil. Scatter the potatoes evenly across the bottom of the roasting pan. Place the lamb on top of the potatoes and roast, uncovered, until the temperature of the lamb reads 140°F (60°C) on an instant-read thermometer, about 45 minutes.

Transfer the lamb from the roasting pan to a cutting board and allow to rest, covered with the reserved foil, for 20 minutes. Place the potatoes in a separate serving dish.

When you're ready to carve the lamb, remove the foil from the resting meat. The bone runs at an angle through the leg, giving you two fairly large pieces of meat on either side to work with. Start on whichever side you feel most comfortable with and slice the meat against the grain into ¼-inch (5 mm) slices.

Lay the sliced lamb over the potatoes in the serving dish and pour any accumulated meat juices over everything before bringing the dish to the table.

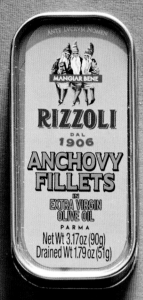

ANTE LVCRVM NOMEN

MANGIAR BENE

RIZZOLI
DAL
1906
ANCHOVY
FILLETS
IN
EXTRA VIRGIN
OLIVE OIL
PARMA
Net Wt 3.17oz (90g)
Drained Wt 1.79 oz (51g)

OLASAGASTI
DELICIAS DEL MAR CANTÁBRICO

FILETES DE ANCHOA
EN ACEITE DE OLIVA

DESDE
1891
CONSERVAS

ORTIZ

El
Velero

ANCHOVIES in olive oil

NET WT.
1.67 oz
(47.5g)

Anchovies in olive oil

WILD
CAUGHT

KEEP
COOL

Ⓤ

Roland®
**FLAT FILLETS
OF ANCHOVIES**
IN OLIVE OIL, SALT ADDED
NET WT. 2 OZ. (57g)

Arte en el Paladar

DON BOCARTE

ANCHOVIES
OF THE GULF OF BISCAY

OLIVE OIL
EXTRA VIRGIN

6/7 FILLETS

SARDINES

CLUPEIDAE

CLOSE YOUR EYES. NOW IMAGINE YOURSELF SITTING ON A patio, the salty smell and warm breeze drifting in off the Atlantic Ocean where it collides with Portugal's Douro River. You sip a glass of crisp white wine and ask your server for the local specialty. He replies, "Certamente!" Only a few minutes pass before a plate with nothing more than fresh bread, a wedge of lemon, and a tin of sardines lands at your table. You take your first bite and realize that these aren't just any tinned sardines.

Portugal is home to arguably the largest tinned seafood culture in the world, and at the heart of this culture is the glorious sardine. Plump, meaty, and with a mild flavor, tinned sardines are the perfect power food. High in protein, omega-3 fatty acids, and B vitamins and vitamin D, as well as several other vitamins and minerals, these little fish make a big impact on the body. Sardines are especially useful for heart health, hormone balance, lowering cholesterol, and red blood cell formation.

In addition to being extremely healthful, they are also one of the most sustainable fish in our oceans. In countries such as Portugal, Spain, France, and Italy, where the waters have long been abundant with fresh sardines, there isn't a better way to eat these fish than grilled with a squeeze of lemon juice. For the rest of the world, however, fresh sardines can be challenging to obtain and are super perishable when they are available, so we turn to the same sardines just stored in a tin for later use.

These tinned sardines are extremely versatile in the kitchen. Their meaty texture and rich flavor allow them to be the star of the show, as in Marinated Sardines and Aioli on Toast (page 63), but they can also be used as a building block in a harmonious flavor explosion, as is evident in Spaghetti con le Sarde (page 61).

WHAT'S IN THE TIN

You can find tinned sardines packed in either water or oil. Opt for those packed in oil, which keeps the fish moist and helps carry its rich flavor. Aside from in water and oil, sardines can also be packed with spicy tomato sauce, oil and lemon, oil and chile, and so on. Tinned sardines come skin-on and bone-in. It is perfectly safe to eat both, with the bonus of the bones being rich in calcium. For the recipes in this chapter, use your favorite tinned sardines packed in oil unless noted otherwise.

ESPINALER

— DESDE 1896 —

SPICY

BABY SARDINES
IN OLIVE OIL · SPICY

10/12

Net Weight: 115 g (4 oz)   Drained Net Weight 81 g (3 oz)

Vital Choice
Wild Sardines
in Extra-Virgin Olive Oil

ORTIZ

RECETA
1824
ORIGINAL

El Velero

SARDINAS
A LA ANTIGUA
en aceite de oliva

Elaborado en los
R... ...llegas

PESO NETO: 120g (4.2 OZ)

EST. Roland® 1934

SARDINAS

PESCA SALVAJE

en
ACEITE
DE OLIVA

PESO NETO 4.4 OZ. (125g)

Artisanal Tradition

Sustainably
Caught

PORTUGAL

Santo Amaro
1930

100%
Natural

GLUTEN
FREE

European Sardines
Sardina Pilchardus
in Olive Oil & Red Piri Piri Pepper
Lightly Smoked
Hand-Packed in Portugal

NET WT 4.2 OZ (120g)

Net Wt. 4.4 oz (124g)

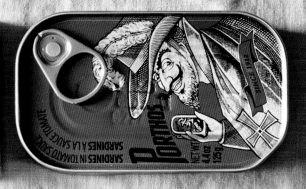

SARDINES IN TOMATO SAUCE
SARDINES À LA SAUCE TOMATE

PORTHOS

SINCE 1920

NET WT.
4.4 OZ
(125g)

CABO de PENAS
GRAN SELECCION

Sardinas
en aceite de oliva

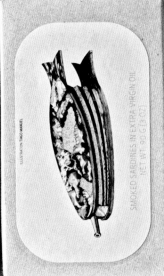

ILLUSTRATION TIAGO MANUEL

SMOKED SARDINES IN EXTRA VIRGIN OIL
NET WT. 90 G (3 OZ)

WILD
SARDINES
IN SPANISH OLIVE OIL

NET WT. 120g (4.2 oz)

Matiz

Wild caught in the Eastern Atlantic

2 grams of Omega-3s per serving and high in Calcium

IMPORTED BY
matiz
Lynnwood, WA 98087
A Culinary Collective Company
www.culinarycollective.com

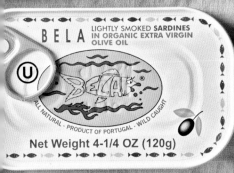

BELA

LIGHTLY SMOKED SARDINES
IN ORGANIC EXTRA VIRGIN
OLIVE OIL

U

BELA®

ALL NATURAL · PRODUCT OF PORTUGAL · WILD CAUGHT

Net Weight 4-1/4 OZ (120g)

PESO NETO: 120g (4.2 OZ)

con
INGREDIENTES
NATURALES

Elaborado en las
Rías Gallegas

CABO
de PEÑAS
GRAN SELECCION

Sugerencia de presentación

Sardinas
en aceite de oliva

SPAGHETTI CON LE SARDE

This Sicilian classic was born in the city of Palermo and shows the influence the Arab rule of the tenth century had over the cuisine of the region. The contrasting salty and sweet flavors paired with the aromatics of fennel and saffron will make this an instant favorite in your pasta repertoire.

SERVES 2

3 tablespoons golden raisins

1 tablespoon panko or other bread crumbs

3 tablespoons olive oil

2 tablespoons pine nuts

1½ tablespoons finely diced yellow onion

½ cup (75 g) finely diced fennel

Kosher salt

6 ounces (170 g) spaghetti or strand pasta of your choice

Small pinch of saffron

2 anchovy fillets

One 4.2-ounce (120 g) tin sardines

Lemon, for squeezing

1½ tablespoons minced fennel fronds

Preheat the oven to 350°F (180°C).

Bring a large pot of water to a boil over high heat for the pasta. This can take up to 20 minutes, depending on your stove. Use this time to gather the rest of your ingredients.

Put the raisins in a dish just big enough to hold them. Cover with warm water and set aside to soak—just long enough to plump up and infuse the water with a bit of flavor, 10 minutes or so. Drain the raisins, reserving 1 tablespoon of the soaking liquid.

Place the panko in a small bowl, toss with 1 tablespoon of the olive oil, and place on one half of a small sheet pan. Scatter the pine nuts on the other half of the pan and place in the heated oven for 10 minutes. Take care to give both the pine nuts and the bread crumbs a gentle stir halfway through. Set aside.

In a skillet, heat the remaining 2 tablespoons olive oil over medium heat until it shimmers a bit. Add the onion and fennel and cook the vegetables until they are just soft but do not brown, 4 to 5 minutes. If you notice a little color on the fennel or onions, add a small pinch of salt. The salt will pull moisture from the vegetables, reducing the chance of browning. Remove from the heat.

Add enough salt to the boiling water so that it reminds you of a less salty sea. Add the pasta and cook according to the package directions, stirring the pasta every 2 minutes or so to ensure that it doesn't stick together. Taste a noodle a minute or so before the end of the suggested cooking time to ensure that your pasta comes out al dente.

To the skillet, add the raisins, the reserved soaking liquid, the toasted pine nuts, saffron, anchovies, and sardines. Scoop out ⅓ cup (80 ml) of the starchy pasta cooking water and add to the pan.

Return the pan to medium-high heat. Drain the pasta, add to the pan, and cook it at an aggressive simmer, making sure you are constantly stirring and tossing. I know the tossing and stirring seems like a bit of extra work, but trust me, this will guarantee a creamier and more cohesive pasta in the end.

When the sauce has reduced just enough to coat the noodles and leave a little extra in the bottom of the pan, squeeze in some lemon juice, add the fennel fronds, and give the pasta one last toss or two. Divide the mixture between two bowls and top with the toasted bread crumbs.

MARINATED SARDINES
AND AIOLI ON TOAST

In this recipe, tinned sardines get quickly marinated in seasoned vinegar. The bite from the marinated fish is a great contrast to the rich aioli, fresh dill, and charred bread. (Be sure to use a good crusty loaf.) But once the sardines have been marinated, they also make a fine addition to a fresh green salad.

SERVES 2

MARINATED SARDINES

1 large clove garlic, thinly sliced

3 tablespoons red wine vinegar

2 tablespoons olive oil

1 sprig thyme, leaves picked

¼ teaspoon chili flakes

One 4.2-ounce (120 g) tin sardines

AIOLI

1 large egg yolk

1 small clove garlic, grated on a Microplane

¼ teaspoon kosher salt

2 teaspoons water

½ cup (120 ml) olive oil

Small pinch of smoked paprika

1½ teaspoons fresh lemon juice

FOR ASSEMBLY

2 slices sourdough bread, charred

6 fresh chives, minced

Freshly ground black pepper

To marinate the sardines: In a small bowl, combine the garlic, vinegar, olive oil, thyme, and chili flakes. Using a fork, smash and stir the ingredients so that you have a fragrant and tasty marinade.

Carefully remove the sardines from their tin, place them in the marinade, and let sit for 20 minutes or so. What you are trying to achieve are sardines that are slightly pickled but remain intact. If they stay in the vinegary marinade for too long, they will begin to turn to mush.

To make the aioli: In a medium bowl, whisk together the egg yolk, garlic, salt, and water until fully incorporated. Whisking constantly, add a teaspoon or so of olive oil (adding very small amounts of olive oil to begin ensures that your emulsion won't break). After a few seconds, add another, and then another. At this point, you should have a nice base emulsion. While you continue to whisk, slowly drizzle in the remaining olive oil. You should be left with a homogenous mixture. Season the aioli with smoked paprika and lemon juice.

To assemble: Spread a generous amount of aioli on the charred bread, top with sardines, and garnish with chives and a few cracks of black pepper.

BEER-BATTERED SARDINES WITH HARISSA

Coating with a beer batter is a classic way to prepare any flaky white-fleshed fish, especially in the United Kingdom. In this recipe, tinned sardines get the same treatment, and the crispy fish make a delicious snack or appetizer. Any leftover harissa, a fiery and smoky pepper sauce with roots in Morocco, can be used with other fried foods, or with roasted vegetables, or drizzled over scrambled eggs. If you can, make the harissa a day ahead of time to give the flavors an opportunity to meld, but it's delicious day-of, too.

SERVES 2

HARISSA

4 roasted red peppers (see Notes)

¼ cup (60 ml) olive oil

2 tablespoons red wine vinegar

2 tablespoons harissa seasoning (see Notes)

BEER-BATTERED SARDINES

Neutral oil, such as grapeseed or canola, for sautéing

1½ cups (190 g) all-purpose flour

½ teaspoon cayenne pepper

One 12-ounce (355 ml) bottle lager beer

Two 4.2-ounce (120 g) tins sardines packed in lemon and oil

Kosher salt

Lemon wedges (optional)

To make the harissa: In a food processor, combine the roasted peppers, olive oil, vinegar, and harissa seasoning and blend until smooth.

To prepare the sardines: Pour 3 inches (8 cm) of neutral oil into a medium saucepan and warm over medium heat. You'll know the oil is ready for the fish when a small pinch of flour bubbles immediately once it hits the oil.

In a large bowl, stir together the flour and cayenne. Add the beer slowly to avoid too much foam. Using a fork, gently stir the mixture. A few clumps are okay; overmixing is not.

Place the sardines in the batter and carefully toss with a spoon to coat. Once you check the temperature of the oil and deem it good to go, lift the sardines one at a time from the batter, allowing excess batter to drip back into the bowl. Do this one by one until you have 6 to 8 sardines in the oil, depending on the size of your pan.

Fry the sardines until golden brown, 2 to 3 minutes. Take care not to overcrowd the pan, as this will drop the temperature of the oil and you'll end up with soggy, greasy fish. Once the fish are cooked, use a slotted spoon to transfer them to a plate lined with paper towels. Season with a bit of salt. Repeat this process until all the sardines are fried.

Divide the sardines between two plates and serve with a dollop of the harissa sauce and a wedge of lemon, if you'd like.

NOTES: You can use store-bought roasted peppers from a jar, or roast fresh peppers yourself over an open flame or under a broiler. You want to get them good and blackened all over. Then set them aside to cool. Peel the peppers and discard the skin. Cut the roasted peppers in half and scrape out any seeds. Use the peppers right away or cover in olive oil and store in your refrigerator for up to a week.

Since harissa seasoning blends can have different levels of heat depending on the brand, taste the spice mix and add more or less, depending on how hot you want the harissa. You could also add a pinch of chili flakes. If you like it mild and prefer less kick, add another roasted pepper.

EST. Roland 1934
SARDINAS
— en —
ACEITE DE OLIVA
PESO NETO 4.4 OZ. (125g)

BOM PETISCO
SARDINHAS
em azeite

ORTIZ
RECETA ORIGINAL 1824
El Velero
SARDINAS
A LA ANTIGUA
en aceite de oliva

Beach Cliff SARDINES
IN LOUISIANA
HOT SAUCE
PRODUCT OF POLAND
LIFT RING TO RING · PULL BACK
INGREDIENTS: SPRATS, WATER, MALTODEXTRIN, ACETIC ACID, SALT, PAPRIKA (COLOR), MODIFIED CORNSTARCH, SPICE EXTRACTIVES (INCLUDING PAPRIKA (COLOR), XANTHAN GUM, POLYSORBATE 80, CARAMEL COLOR. CONTAINS: SPRATS. MAY CONTAIN CRUSTACEANS.
DISTRIBUTED BY: BUMBLE BEE SEAFOODS, SAN DIEGO, CA 92186 USA FOR NUTRITION FACTS, WRITE TO THE ADDRESS LISTED
NET WT 3.75 oz (106 g)   www.beachcliff.info
0 20100 00019 9

great taste 2016
TOP 100 MUNDIAL
La Brújula
CONSERVAS ARTESANAS
SARDINAS
Nº 31
EN ACEITE DE OLIVA
SARDINILLAS
16/20 PIEZAS

BOM PETISCO
SARDINHAS
em tomate

SARDINES ON RYE WITH BIBB LETTUCE, RED ONION, AND AVOCADO

This sandwich is as simple as it is delicious. An updated version of a New York City classic, it gets a Scandinavian twist with the addition of crème fraîche. You could also serve this sandwich open-faced; lose the top slice of bread and add a fried egg for a quick breakfast.

MAKES 2 SANDWICHES

4 tablespoons (55 g) crème fraîche

2 tablespoons yellow mustard

4 slices rye bread, toasted or not (it's up to you!)

One 4.2-ounce (120 g) tin sardines

1 avocado, thinly sliced

⅓ small red onion, thinly sliced into rings

¼ cup (35 g) thinly sliced cucumber

6 leaves Bibb lettuce (you can substitute any lettuce you have on hand)

3 sprigs dill, fronds picked in small bunches

In a small bowl, stir together the crème fraîche and mustard. Spread the mustard mixture evenly over the 4 slices of bread.

Dividing the ingredients evenly, layer them on one piece of bread in this order: sardines, avocado, onion, cucumber, lettuce, and dill. Top with a second piece of bread.

BREAD

YELLOW MUSTARD

CRÈME FRAÎCHE

DILL

BIBB LETTUCE

CUCUMBER

RED ONION

AVOCADO

SARDINES

CRÈME FRAÎCHE

YELLOW MUSTARD

BREAD

DEVILED EGGS WITH SARDINES

The classic deviled egg is one of the all-time great party snacks. Creamy and protein packed, the egg is a wonderful canvas for all sorts of things from bacon and jalapeño to . . . you guessed it, tinned sardines. Choose a tin with chili peppers for added flavor; you can pick a regular tin if heat isn't for you. These deviled eggs are elevated with fresh herbs and a bit of lemon juice to brighten up the rich appetizer.

MAKES 12 DEVILED EGGS

6 large eggs

3 tablespoons mayonnaise

1 tablespoon unsalted butter, at room temperature

2 teaspoons yellow mustard

1 teaspoon minced fresh tarragon

1 tablespoon minced fresh chives

Lemon, for squeezing

Kosher salt and freshly ground black pepper

One 3.5-ounce (100 g) tin sardines with chili peppers

Hot sauce

Find a pot large enough to fit the eggs in a single layer and fill it with enough water to cover the eggs by about 2 inches (5 cm), but don't put the eggs in yet. Bring the water to a boil over high heat. Using a slotted spoon or mesh skimmer, gently lower the eggs into the water. Reduce the heat and bring the water from a boil to a simmer, then set a timer for 11 minutes. Keep an eye out for any eggs that crack during the first few seconds. If one does, not to worry; scoop it out and replace with an intact one.

Use this time to prepare an ice bath by filling a medium bowl with equal parts ice and water. Gather the rest of your ingredients.

When the timer goes off, use a slotted spoon to carefully transfer the eggs to the ice bath and allow to rest for 6 minutes or until the eggs are cool enough to handle with your hands. Peel the eggs. This technique for cooking the eggs should have yielded great results for easy-to-peel eggs. It always helps to crack the eggs on the butt of the shell where an air pocket forms during cooking. If you do run into a little trouble removing the shells, try peeling the eggs under running water.

Continued

Once the eggs are peeled, slice them in half lengthwise and scoop out the yolks into a medium bowl. Place the whites on a plate lined with paper towels to catch any water left from the peeling process.

With a fork, give the egg yolks a good mashing until they are relatively smooth. Add the mayonnaise, butter, and mustard. Using the fork, you should be able mash the yolks a bit smoother while incorporating the added ingredients. Stir in the tarragon and chives. Season with a squeeze of lemon juice and salt and pepper to taste.

To serve, use two small spoons to fill the egg whites with the yolk filling. (It's easiest to scoop with one spoon while using the other to guide the filling.) Once all the eggs are filled, top with the sardines. Depending on the size of the sardines in your tin, you may need to break them into inch-long (2.5 cm) pieces. Splash a little hot sauce on each egg and arrange the eggs on your favorite plate; enjoy immediately.

SARDINES IN A PINCH

On a day when you find yourself hungry and need a fast, delicious, and hearty snack, try sardines and crackers. It takes only a few ingredients that you probably already have on hand. It's also a great meal to pack and eat on the go.

Wasa crispbreads or saltine crackers

Whole-grain mustard

1 tin sardines

Lemon, for squeezing

Spread the crispbread with mustard, top with sardines, and squeeze some lemon juice over the top.

FUSILLI WITH SARDINES, 'NDUJA, AND PECORINO

What is 'nduja, you ask? It's a spicy spreadable salume that originates in Calabria. Once a rare find outside of Italy, 'nduja is starting to pop up stateside. You can find it in local cheese shops or in better markets. It can be used as part of an antipasto board, slathered on pizza, and, as in this case, added to pasta. The finished dish is the perfect combination of land and sea.

SERVES 2

3 tablespoons 'nduja

½ cup (130 g) tomato puree

One 4.2-ounce (120 g) tin sardines

Kosher salt

6 ounces (170 g) fusilli

3½ tablespoons unsalted butter

2 teaspoons red wine vinegar

5 leaves fresh basil, torn into smaller pieces, plus more for garnish

4 tablespoons (25 g) grated pecorino cheese

Bring a large pot of water to a boil over high heat for the pasta. This can take up to 20 minutes, depending on your stove. Use this time to gather the rest of your ingredients.

Heat a skillet over medium-high heat. When the pan is warm, add the 'nduja. Use the back of a wooden spoon or silicone spatula to flatten the 'nduja. What you want here is something that looks like a thin sausage patty. By getting color on one side, you'll intensify the flavor without losing the integrity of the sausage.

Add the tomato puree and reduce the heat to medium. Slowly cook the tomato/'nduja mixture until the tomato sauce has taken on the flavor of the sausage, about 5 minutes. Add the sardines and use your spoon or spatula to break them into large pieces (as you continue to cook the sauce with the pasta, the sardines will turn into smaller pieces, ensuring a bit in each bite). Remove the pan from the heat.

Add enough salt to the boiling water so that it reminds you of a less salty sea. Add the pasta and cook according to the package directions, stirring the pasta every

2 minutes or so to ensure that it doesn't stick together. Taste a noodle a minute or so before the end of the suggested cooking time to ensure that your pasta comes out al dente.

About a minute before the pasta is ready to come out of the pot, add about ¼ cup (60 ml) of the pasta cooking water to the sauce and return the sauce to a hard simmer. Drain the pasta, add to the pan, and cook at an aggressive simmer, making sure you are constantly stirring and tossing. I know the tossing and stirring seems like a bit of extra work, but trust me, this will guarantee a creamier and more cohesive pasta in the end.

When the sauce has reduced by three-quarters, stir in the butter until it is completely melted and emulsified into the sauce. Add the vinegar and torn basil. Give the pan a few tosses before you stir in 3 tablespoons of the pecorino.

Divide the pasta between two bowls and garnish with the remaining cheese and basil.

SARDINE, BEAN, AND ESCAROLE SOUP

A good soup is the true measure of any seasoned cook. This is because soups are deceptively simple to make but require a delicate touch to balance the flavors. And this soup is guaranteed to impress without forcing you to spend all day putting it together. To make it a bit heartier and more filling, serve it over a piece of yesterday's bread toasted up until crispy.

SERVES 4

1½ tablespoons olive oil

1½ cups (190 g) finely diced yellow onion

1 cup (150 g) finely diced fennel

4 cloves garlic, minced

1 head escarole, cut into 1-inch (2.5 cm) pieces (about 4 cups/150 g)

Two 15-ounce (425 g) cans white beans

1 cup (240 g) canned whole tomatoes, hand-crushed

2 teaspoons fresh thyme, chopped

4 cups (1 L) stock (I prefer chicken, but vegetable works well, too)

Two 4.2-ounce (120 g) tins sardines

¼ teaspoon smoked paprika

Kosher salt and freshly ground black pepper

1½ teaspoons sherry vinegar

Crusty bread, for serving

In a 6-quart (5.5 L) saucepot or your favorite soup pot, heat the olive oil over medium-high heat until it shimmers. Add the onion and fennel and sweat until soft, 5 or 6 minutes. Add the garlic and cook until fragrant, 2 or 3 minutes. Add the escarole and cook until it begins to wilt, 3 to 4 minutes.

Now that you've made the base for the soup, gently stir in the beans, crushed tomatoes, and thyme until the thyme is evenly dispersed and its subtle aroma lifts from the pot. Add the stock and bring the soup to a simmer. Cover the pot, reduce the heat just a bit to medium, and cook for about 10 minutes to warm the soup through.

Uncover and taste your work thus far. Good? Yes. Fantastic? Not quite. Add the sardines, smoked paprika, salt and pepper to taste, and the vinegar. Give the soup a quick stir and ladle it into your best bowls, over a piece of crusty bread, if you'd like.

SARDINE PO'BOY

Po'boys are a classic New Orleans sandwich stuffed with meat or fish. The bread for a po'boy is crucial. Make sure you get an airy and flaky loaf of New Orleans–style French bread (which is nothing like French bread from France). Any hot sauce could work here, but Crystal brand will give you the most authentic Louisiana flavor. Eat your po'boy with a cold beer for a truly satisfying meal.

MAKES 2 SANDWICHES

RÉMOULADE

1 cup (225 g) mayonnaise

4 tablespoons (60 g) Dijon mustard

2 tablespoons prepared horseradish

2 tablespoons chopped fresh parsley

2 cloves garlic, minced

1 tablespoon white wine vinegar

1 teaspoon hot sauce

1 tablespoon Old Bay Seasoning

1 tablespoon (15 grams) chopped capers

PO'BOYS

Two 8-inch (20 cm) loaves French bread (see headnote)

Three 4.2-ounce (120 g) tins sardines

2 red radishes, thinly sliced

2 scallions, thinly sliced

1 tomato, thinly sliced

Handful of sliced dill pickles

Handful of shredded iceberg lettuce

Lemon, for squeezing

To make the rémoulade: In a bowl, stir together the mayonnaise, mustard, horseradish, parsley, garlic, vinegar, hot sauce, Old Bay, and capers and stir to combine. That's it! You can use the rémoulade for up to 3 days; it's also a great dip for fried snacks.

To assemble the po'boys: Split open the bread and spread both cut sides generously with the rémoulade. Dividing them evenly between the sandwiches, layer the ingredients in this order (to maximize both flavor and texture): sardines (making sure to cover as much of the bread as possible), radishes, scallions, tomato, pickles, and lettuce. Top with a squeeze of lemon juice. Building the sandwich this way ensures a crispy start and finish and keeps that delicious sardine flavor around until the next bite!

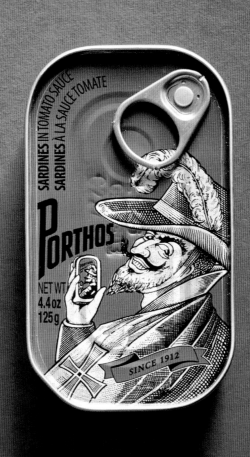

SARDINES ON A BOARD

Creating a vibrant mix of ingredients and presenting them on a board is one of my favorite ways to entertain with tinned fish—especially with sardines. The method is simple: Pop open a few tins and pull some of your favorite accompaniments from the cupboard and fridge. There are no rules on what makes a good appetizing board; experiment with a mix of different flavors and textures. Here are some of my favorite additions.

A selection of different-flavored sardines (plan on one tin per person for a hungry crowd)

Sliced baguette

Butter

Saltines

Potato chips

Sour cream

Mayonnaise

Spicy mustard

Horseradish cream

Fresh herbs

Flaky sea salt

Pickles (the more the merrier)

Avocado slices

Shaved red onion

Shaved fennel

Lemon wedges

Shaved jalapeño

Shaved cucumbers

Olives

Almonds

Capers

Halved radishes

MACKEREL

SCOMBRIDAE

THE WORD *MACKEREL* DERIVES FROM THE LATIN WORD *MACULA*, meaning "marked" or "spotted." It's these beautiful markings that make this fish so recognizable around the world with its blue, bordering on teal, skin striped in black. Aside from their distinct appearance, mackerel are known for being a healthful and very sustainable seafood option.

Tinned mackerel is an excellent source of protein and is high in omega-3s and rich in vitamin K, which is essential for heart health and aids in lowering blood pressure and cholesterol levels. Mackerel is also rich in vitamin B_{12}, vitamin D, and vitamin E. These vitamins help with healthy skin, boosting the immune system, and minimizing the effects of arthritis and inflammation in the body.

Atlantic mackerel is a saltwater fish that is richer and milder in taste than tuna. Which means tinned mackerel is a great substitute in any recipe that calls for canned tuna. Tuna has become overfished in recent years and is mostly unregulated in many places across the globe, which is why the world's population of tuna is shrinking (and why I didn't include any tuna recipes in this book). So reach for mackerel instead; most anything you make with tuna can be made equally delicious with mackerel. With that in mind, try Roasted Pork Loin with "Tonnato" Sauce (page 114), which is reminiscent of the same dish that's usually made with veal and tuna. Mackerel on toast makes a healthful lunch or breakfast, and mackerel as an addition to a salad is a natural choice.

WHAT'S IN THE TIN

Tinned mackerel comes from many different countries and is prepared in a variety of ways. You can find the fish bone-in or boneless, skin-on or skinless, and packed in a wide range of sauces. For the recipes in this book, you should use boneless/ skinless mackerel packed in olive oil, unless noted otherwise.

If your tinned mackerel fillets contain bones, they may be soft enough to eat. If not, they can be removed by simply pulling them out with your fingers. The same process is used for the skin. Remove and discard before proceeding with the recipe.

You'll find mackerel packed in water or brine but also flavored with tomato sauce, chili, mustard, or even soy sauce. I suggest you try them all and after cooking through a recipe at least once, substitute your favorite flavor to put your own spin on it.

MACKEREL ESCABECHE
ON TOAST

Escabeche is a classic Spanish technique that uses a hot liquid of oil and vinegar to cook anything from seafood to vegetables. Here it is used more as a marinade to infuse the tinned mackerel with a pickled flavor. If you have leftover liquid, use it to season a pot of braised greens for the added umami flavor.

SERVES 2

¼ cup (60 ml) grapeseed or other neutral oil

¼ cup (60 ml) olive oil

¼ cup (60 ml) champagne vinegar or other white wine vinegar

1 clove garlic, smashed

¼ small red onion, thinly sliced

1 bay leaf

3 sprigs thyme

One 4.4-ounce (125 g) tin mackerel

FOR ASSEMBLY

2 tablespoons unsalted butter, at room temperature

2 slices sourdough bread

2 tablespoons toasted pine nuts

2 teaspoons smoked paprika

Small handful of fresh parsley

Pinch of flaky sea salt, such as Maldon

In a small saucepot, combine the grapeseed oil, olive oil, vinegar, garlic, onion, bay leaf, and thyme. Bring to a boil over medium-high heat. Remove from the heat and let steep for 30 minutes. Allowing the contents of the pot to steep not only gives the ingredients time to meld together but also gives the oil time to cool just a bit before being poured over the mackerel that is already cooked.

While the escabeche liquid is steeping, carefully remove the mackerel fillets from the tin and place them in a small baking dish or other dish large enough to arrange them side by side in a single layer.

Pour the escabeche liquid over the mackerel and let rest for another 30 minutes. Again, you want the flavors to meld. This time, though, you want the vinegary/herby liquid from the pot to infuse the mackerel.

Meanwhile, preheat the oven to 400°F (200°C).

To assemble the toasts: Spread 1 tablespoon of butter on each slice of bread, making sure to coat both sides of the bread evenly. Put the buttered bread on a baking sheet and cook until hot and crispy on the edges but still a bit soft toward the center, 5 to 7 minutes.

Remove the toasts from the oven and transfer them to a cutting board. Divide the mackerel between the 2 slices of toast. Fish out some of the onions and drape them over the mackerel. Sprinkle the toasted pine nuts evenly over the toast, sprinkle evenly with the smoked paprika, and top with a bit of parsley. Using a small spoon, drizzle a small amount of the escabeche liquid over the parsley for a little added zing and top with a pinch of flaky salt.

MACKEREL AND POACHED EGG ON TOAST

Learning to poach eggs will serve you for many years to come. It may take you a time or two to get the poaching right (see technique, below), but before long, you'll master the firm whites and runny yolks that are the hallmarks of the perfectly poached eggs coveted by most brunch aficionados. For a new way to enjoy poached eggs, try them over toast with mackerel fillets in mustard.

MAKES 4 TOASTS

2 tablespoons distilled white vinegar

4 thick slices sourdough bread, about 1 inch (2.5 cm) thick

¼ cup (60 ml) olive oil

1 tablespoon Dijon mustard

½ cup (120 g) sour cream

Kosher salt and freshly ground black pepper

4 large eggs, the fresher the better

Two 4.4-ounce (125 g) tins mackerel in whole-grain mustard

Small handful of arugula or watercress

Lemon, for squeezing

Fill a small saucepot three-quarters of the way with water. Add the vinegar and bring to a boil. The vinegar will help the egg whites hold their shape.

While waiting for the water to come to a boil, drizzle both sides of the 4 slices of bread evenly with the olive oil. Toast the bread under your broiler or on a griddle. You want some color but still want the bread to be soft in the middle. In a small bowl, mix together the mustard and sour cream. Season with salt and pepper.

Turn the water down to a gentle simmer. One at a time, crack an egg into a small bowl and carefully slide the egg into the water. Gently give the water a stir two or three times. This helps the eggs to cook evenly. Allow the eggs to simmer for 3 minutes for runny yolks or 5 minutes if you prefer them a bit firmer.

Evenly spread the mustard mixture on the toasted bread. Top each piece of toast with a half tin of mackerel. Using a slotted spoon, remove the eggs one at a time and place one on each piece of toast and season with salt and pepper. Top with a few leaves of arugula or cress, squeeze on a little lemon juice, and serve.

SMOKED MACKEREL SALAD WITH BEETS, HORSERADISH, AND CRÈME FRAÎCHE

This salad has a little bit of everything good: sweet and earthy beets, smoky mackerel, and punchy horseradish. The salad can be plated in a way to impress, but it is equally delicious quickly tossed together in a bowl or packed in a container for lunch.

SERVES 2

8 to 10 baby beets, well scrubbed

2 teaspoons plus 1 tablespoon olive oil

Kosher salt and freshly ground black pepper

Lemon, for squeezing

½ cup (110 g) crème fraîche

1 tablespoon minced fresh chives, plus more for garnish

One 3.8-ounce (110 g) tin smoked mackerel, plain or peppered

1-inch (2.5 cm) piece fresh horseradish, peeled

Preheat the oven to 350°F (180°C).

In a medium bowl, drizzle the beets with 2 teaspoons of the olive oil. Season liberally with salt and pepper and toss to coat.

Place a small baking sheet on your countertop and place a sheet of foil on top of the baking sheet. Place the seasoned beets in the center of the foil in a single layer. Fold all the edges of the foil toward the center, fold again, and crimp closed. Your goal is to have an airtight pouch for the beets to cook in.

Place the baking sheet in the oven and bake until the beets are slightly soft when you give them a squeeze through the foil, about 50 minutes. The pouch will be a bit warm, so use caution doing this. Remove from the oven, carefully vent the pouch, and allow to cool.

When the beets are cool enough to handle, peel them. (If the beets are red, either wear gloves or be okay with a getting a little red tint on your hands. Beets are actually used to dye all sorts of things such as cookie icing, clothing, and even hair.)

Continued

You can use an old kitchen towel or a sturdy paper towel to simply rub the outside of the beets until all the skin has been removed. As you work, place the beets in a medium bowl. Season with a small pinch of salt, a crack or two of black pepper, and a squeeze of lemon juice.

In a small bowl, stir or whisk together the crème fraîche, chives, and the remaining 1 tablespoon olive oil.

To serve, grab two salad plates and use the back of a spoon to spread crème fraîche evenly on each. Place the beets on top of the crème fraîche and top with pieces of the smoked mackerel. Using a Microplane, grate the fresh horseradish over the beets and mackerel. No need to be exact here; a little on the rim of the plate will make for a nice presentation. Garnish with chives and enjoy.

MACKEREL CAKES WITH
CABBAGE AND CILANTRO

Mackerel cakes are super quick to put together. They get a blast of flavor from ginger and Korean chili paste, and they pair perfectly with the crunchy cabbage and tangy yogurt dressing. Mackerel cakes are a great make-ahead meal to freeze so that you can have them on hand whenever a craving strikes.

MAKES 6 LARGE OR 12 SMALL CAKES

MACKEREL CAKES

Two 4.4-ounce (125 g) tins mackerel

2 large eggs

2 cloves garlic, grated finely with a Microplane

1 tablespoon grated fresh ginger (grated with a Microplane)

1 tablespoon gochujang, preferably Mother in Law's brand

½ cup (30 g) thinly sliced scallions

3 tablespoons finely chopped fresh cilantro

3 tablespoons panko bread crumbs

Kosher salt

CABBAGE

1 cup (95 g) thinly sliced green cabbage

1 tablespoon yogurt

Juice of ½ lime

2 tablespoons thinly sliced scallion greens

¼ cup (7 g) fresh cilantro with a bit of stem attached

Kosher salt

2 tablespoons neutral oil, such as canola

Kosher salt

Gochujang, preferably Mother in Law's brand

Fresh cilantro

1 lime, cut into 4 wedges

To make the mackerel cakes: Place the mackerel in a medium bowl and flake it apart with a fork. Crack in the eggs and thoroughly mix with the mackerel. Add the garlic, ginger, gochujang, scallions, cilantro, and panko. Again, thoroughly mix, making sure that all the ingredients are dispersed evenly. Season with salt.

If you are making a meal for two, divide the mixture into six equal portions and roll into balls. If using the cakes as snacks, form the mixture into balls the size of a golf ball. Turn the balls into round patties, set them on a plate, and place them in the refrigerator.

Continued

To prepare the cabbage: In a medium bowl, combine the cabbage, yogurt, and lime juice. Gently massage the cabbage until it is completely coated in the yogurt and lime. Mix in the scallion greens and cilantro. Season with salt.

Pour the neutral oil into a skillet and place over medium-high heat. Remove the mackerel patties from the refrigerator and place as many as you can in the pan without overcrowding. Cook until the cakes are hot throughout and beautifully browned and crispy on the outside, 2 to 3 minutes on each side for the larger cakes, a little less for the snack-size cakes. Remove the cakes from the pan to a plate lined with a paper towel to drain. Sprinkle with a little salt.

Divide the cabbage evenly between two plates, top with the mackerel cakes, and garnish with gochujang, cilantro, and lime wedges.

MACKEREL, GREEN BEAN, AND TOMATO SALAD WITH CHORIZO VINAIGRETTE

This mackerel salad makes the perfect lunch. The vinaigrette gets a smoky element from the Spanish chorizo and pimenton; it goes great with the mackerel and snappy green beans.

SERVES 2

CHORIZO VINAIGRETTE

2 tablespoons olive oil

3 ounces (85 g) cooked Spanish chorizo (see Note)

½ teaspoon dried oregano

1½ tablespoons sherry vinegar

SALAD

6 ounces (170 g) green beans

¼ cup (20 g) thinly sliced red onion

8 cherry tomatoes, halved

One 4.4-ounce (125 g) tin mackerel

¼ cup (35 g) Marcona almonds, roughly chopped

¼ cup (7 g) torn fresh basil

Kosher salt and freshly ground black pepper

To make the vinaigrette: In a skillet, warm the olive oil over medium heat. Add the chorizo and cook until it browns; break up any large clumps. Add the oregano and cook for 1 minute. Remove the pan from the heat and pour in the vinegar.

For the salad: Bring a pot of salted water to a boil over high heat. Fill a large bowl with ice water. Add the green beans to the boiling water and cook for 3 minutes. Immediately transfer the beans to the ice bath and completely cool. Remove the beans from the ice bath and let air-dry on a clean kitchen towel.

In a medium bowl, combine the green beans, onion, tomatoes, mackerel, half of the almonds, the basil, and the chorizo vinaigrette. Gently mix, taking care to keep the mackerel as chunky as possible. Season with salt and pepper. Sprinkle with the remaining almonds before serving.

NOTE: Use cooked chorizo; try the one from Despaña (see Resources, page 196).

FETTUCCINE WITH MACKEREL, SUN GOLD TOMATOES, AND PARMESAN

This pasta is perfect for when summer is at its peak and tomatoes from the market are sweet and juicy. It gets an umami punch from both the tinned mackerel and the Parmesan cheese. There is nothing sadder than pregrated Parmesan cheese, so splurge for a chunk. Grate it over the fettuccine before serving, using the small holes on a box grater or a Microplane.

SERVES 2

Kosher salt

6 ounces (170 g) fettuccine

1 tablespoon olive oil

1 cup (145 g) Sun Gold tomatoes, halved

One 4.4-ounce (125 g) tin mackerel

2 tablespoons unsalted butter

1 heaping tablespoon thinly sliced fresh basil

Juice of ½ lemon

3 tablespoons grated Parmesan cheese

Bring a large pot of water to a boil over high heat for the pasta. This can take up to 20 minutes, depending on your stove. Use this time to gather the rest of your ingredients.

Add enough salt to the boiling water so that it reminds you of a less salty sea. Add the pasta and cook according to the package directions, stirring the pasta every 2 minutes or so to ensure that it doesn't stick together. Taste a noodle a minute or so before the end of the suggested cooking time to ensure that your pasta comes out al dente.

In a skillet, heat the olive oil over medium-high heat until hot but not smoking. As soon as the oil reaches its smoke point, carefully add the tomatoes. (All liquid fats including olive oil have a smoke point; some oils have higher smoke points than others, which means some are better for cooking at higher temperatures.) Cook the tomatoes for 2 minutes, tossing every 20 seconds or so. Add ¼ cup (60 ml) of the pasta cooking water and remove the pan from the heat. Using the back of a fork, press down on the tomatoes. You are trying to get most of the juice out of the tomatoes to lay the foundation for the sauce.

Drain the pasta and add it to the pan of simmering tomato sauce. Stir the pasta into the sauce and reduce the sauce by three-quarters, giving the pan a few flips along the way. Add the mackerel, taking care to keep the fillets whole.

Remove the pan from the heat and add the butter and basil. Stir and flip the pasta in the pan until the butter is melted, the mackerel fillets have begun to fall apart, and the sauce is emulsified. Squeeze in the lemon juice, add 2 tablespoons of the Parmesan, and stir until incorporated.

Divide the pasta between two bowls and sprinkle with the remaining 1 tablespoon Parmesan.

patagonia
PROVISIONS®

LEMON CAPER
MACKEREL
in olive oil

NET WT 4.2 OZ (120g)

LOT:L14.P BEST BY: MAY 2023

MACKEREL FILLETS IN OLIVE OIL   NET WT: 125 G (4 OZ)

TERESA LIMA

Conservas Santos

Carapaus em Azeite

Fabrico Tradicional Algarvio
Algarve - Olhão

Horse Mackerel in Olive Oil
Chinchards à l'Huile d'Olive
Product of Portugal/Produit du Portugal

VitalChoice
WILD SEAFOOD & ORGANICS

Wild Mackerel
in Extra-Virgin Olive Oil

Net Wt. 4.4 oz (124g)

SINCE 1942
MINERVA®
PASTA DE
CAVALA COM
MALAGUETAS
MACKEREL PATE
WITH CHILLIES

Peso líquido
Net weight
75g

MORGADA

Portuguese Mackerel
in olive oil

Net weight: 4.2 oz

PRODUCT OF PORTUGAL

MACKEREL,
IN PLACE OF TUNA,
SALAD

Nothing seems to scream tinned fish more than a traditional tuna salad. Unfortunately, most canned tuna is not caught in a sustainable way, and the tuna populations all over the world reflect this. So skip the tuna salad and make a mackerel salad instead. No flavor is lost, and you can feel good knowing that with this one easy swap, you are playing a small part in protecting our planet.

SERVES 2

1 stalk celery, finely diced

½ cucumber, finely diced

¼ small red onion, finely diced

1 jalapeño, minced

Kosher salt

2 tablespoons olive oil

1 tablespoon Dijon mustard

½ cup (115 g) mayonnaise

1 tablespoon minced fresh chives

1 tablespoon minced fresh dill

1 tablespoon minced fresh tarragon

Grated zest and juice of ½ lemon

Freshly ground black pepper

Two 4.2-ounce (120 g) tins mackerel
  in piri piri sauce

In a medium bowl, combine the celery, cucumber, onion, and jalapeño. Add a small pinch of salt, mix, and let sit for 5 minutes. This time allows the salt to pull moisture from the vegetables, making the salad, well, less watery. After the 5 minutes, drain off the liquid.

Mix in the olive oil, mustard, mayonnaise, chives, dill, tarragon, lemon zest, and lemon juice. Season with salt and pepper. Fold in the mackerel fillets until well incorporated. Taste and reseason if necessary. The salad will keep for 3 days.

WHAT TO DO WITH MACKEREL SALAD

Mackerel salad is delicious on its own or piled into lettuce cups, but you can never go wrong serving it in a sandwich. There are so many ways to use it.

AS A MELT
One slice of white bread, topped with mackerel salad, sliced red onion, bread-and-butter pickles, and a slice of American cheese. Broil until browned and bubbling.

AS A BREAKFAST SANDWICH
A toasted English muffin, topped with mackerel salad, sliced avocado, a squeeze of lime juice, chili flakes, and scallions.

AS A "LOX" SANDWICH
A split and toasted everything bagel topped with a schmear of cream cheese, mackerel salad, sliced red onion, sliced tomato, sliced cucumber, and bean sprouts.

GIGANTE BEAN AND MACKEREL PLAKI

Inexpensive, filling, and, more important, delicious, plaki is a Greek dish of fresh fish cooked in a flavorful tomato sauce. This recipe honors the tradition by using tinned mackerel but also includes delicious gigante beans, which makes the dish hearty and substantial. If you have a difficult time tracking down gigante beans, lima or corona beans will yield fantastic results as well.

SERVES 2

½ pound (225 g) dried gigante beans, soaked overnight in plenty of water

3 tablespoons olive oil

1 large clove garlic, minced

1 small red onion, finely diced

1 stalk celery, finely diced

½ cup (25 g) chopped fresh parsley

1 bay leaf

1 tablespoon paprika

One 28-ounce (795 g) can crushed tomatoes

One 4.4-ounce (125 g) tin mackerel in tomato sauce (mackerel in oil is a good substitute, but be sure to strain off the oil)

Kosher salt

2 tablespoons crumbled feta cheese

1 tablespoon minced fresh chives

Freshly ground black pepper

Rinse the soaked beans under cold water and place in a soup pot. Add enough cold water to cover the beans by about 3 inches (8 cm). Bring to a boil over high heat, then immediately reduce the heat to a gentle simmer and cook until the beans are easily crushed with the back of a fork, about 1 hour.

Meanwhile, in a deep skillet, combine 1 tablespoon of the olive oil and the garlic and slowly heat over medium heat until the garlic becomes fragrant. This will take a minute or two. Add the onion, celery, parsley, bay leaf, and paprika and cook until all the vegetables soften, about 5 minutes.

Remove the pan from the heat and carefully add the crushed tomatoes. (Maybe it's because they're red and love to stain clothing, but tomatoes have a tendency to splatter if not looked after.) Return the pan to the stove and simmer over medium heat for 10 minutes. Stir in the mackerel and remove from the heat.

Continued

When the beans have become tender, remove from the heat, season with salt, and allow them to rest for 20 minutes or so. You'll want to season so that the bean liquid tastes like a delicious soup. (I always save any leftover bean liquid to use as a base for soup.)

Meanwhile, preheat the oven to 375°F (190°C).

Reserving the cooking liquid, drain the beans and transfer to a baking dish that allows for an inch (2.5 cm) or so of space above the assembled plaki. Pour in ½ cup (120 ml) of the reserved bean liquid, the remaining 2 tablespoons olive oil, and the tomato mixture.

Transfer the baking dish to the oven and bake, uncovered and undisturbed, for 30 minutes. Open the oven and give the beans a quick stir and cook for another 15 minutes. At this point, the beans will have absorbed all the wonderful flavors and the sauce will have thickened.

Sprinkle with the feta, minced chives, and freshly ground pepper before serving.

MACKEREL PAN BAGNAT

Pan bagnat means "bathed bread," and the crusty baguette in this sandwich is crucial to its success. The crust allows the sandwich to hold its shape while soaking up the mackerel juices. Creating a shallow "trough" in the bottom piece of bread by removing some of the crumb ensures that all of your ingredients will fit snugly and you won't have to worry about them spilling out.

SERVES 2

Juice of ½ lemon

2 tablespoons olive oil

2 teaspoons Dijon mustard

8 anchovy fillets, finely chopped

2 teaspoons capers, finely chopped

1 clove garlic, finely chopped

½ cup (70 g) sliced olives (preferably Niçoise, but any will do)

¼ cup (35 g) finely chopped red onion

½ cup (160 g) roasted red pepper strips

3 tablespoons roughly chopped fresh parsley

Two 4.4-ounce (125 g) tins mackerel, oil included

½ crusty French baguette

½ cup (15 g) fresh basil

2 hard-boiled eggs, sliced into 4 pieces each

In a medium bowl, with a fork, stir together the lemon juice, olive oil, and mustard to emulsify. This is an important step to make sure that your sandwich doesn't get greasy.

Add the anchovies, capers, garlic, olives, onion, roasted red peppers, parsley, and mackerel to the emulsion. Mix with a fork so that everything is dispersed evenly. It's okay if the mackerel remains a bit chunky; it will give the final sandwich a better texture.

Slice the baguette horizontally in half. Pull a little of the bread out of the center of the bottom half, creating a trough of sorts. Line the trough with the basil leaves and spoon in the mackerel mixture. Lay the hard-boiled-egg slices across the top and cover with the top piece of the baguette.

Wrap the sandwich tightly in plastic wrap. Press the sandwich by placing it on a plate with a cast-iron pan or other heavy object on top. Place in the refrigerator, weighted down, for at least 4 hours but preferably overnight. Remove from the refrigerator, unwrap, and slice in half.

ROASTED PORK LOIN
WITH "TONNATO" SAUCE

Vitello tonnato, the classic Piedmontese dish of boiled veal served cold with a sauce made from tuna and anchovies, is the inspiration behind this recipe. Mackerel swaps in beautifully for the tuna; roasted pork loin with crispy skin is used in place of veal. Take your time with this dish and pay careful attention to the temperature of the cooked pork because once you pull the pork out of the oven, it will continue to cook.

SERVES 4

ROAST PORK

2 pounds (900 g) boneless pork loin with skin

1 tablespoon olive oil

Kosher salt and freshly ground black pepper

1 tablespoon fennel seeds

"TONNATO" SAUCE

Two 4.4-ounce (125 g) tins mackerel

4 anchovy fillets

1 jalapeño, seeded and minced

1 clove garlic, smashed

1 tablespoon capers

Juice of 2 lemons

½ cup (115 g) mayonnaise

¼ cup (60 ml) olive oil

Lemon wedges, for serving

To prepare the pork: Place the pork roast skin side up on a cutting board and pat the skin dry with a paper towel. With your sharpest knife, score the skin crosswise, making slits about ¼ inch (5 mm) apart, taking extra care not to cut into the flesh below. This is crucial for crispy skin!

To ensure that your pork roast cooks evenly, it is wise to tie it with butcher's twine. Nothing fancy is required here; just cut yourself five pieces of string long enough to fit around the pork, then starting at one end and working your way to the other, simply tie each piece of string around the pork in equal segments. Be careful not to tie it too tight or the meat will bulge and defeat the purpose. Use as much pressure as you would to tie your shoes snugly.

Continued

Rub the olive oil all over the flesh of the roast. Season the roast liberally with salt and pepper. Wait 5 minutes and season with the fennel seed. (The meat will start to sweat after a few minutes, and that helps the fennel seeds stick.)

Line a sheet pan large enough to hold the pork roast with foil and place a rack on top. The foil will make cleanup much more pleasant as well as catch any juices from the pork during cooking. Set the pork on the sheet pan skin side up to rest for 1 hour.

Meanwhile, preheat the oven to 475°F (250°C).

To make the "tonnato" sauce: In a food processor, combine the mackerel, anchovies, jalapeño, garlic, capers, and lemon juice. Pulse 10 to 12 times so that everything becomes a cohesive paste of sorts. Add the mayonnaise and blend until smooth. With the machine running, slowly drizzle in the olive oil.

Pat the pork roast dry. Place in the oven and roast for 25 minutes. Reduce the temperature to 350°F (180°C) and cook until the center of the roast reads 140°F (60°C) on an instant-read thermometer, another 40 to 50 minutes, rotating the pan from front to back halfway through. Let the roast rest for at least 15 minutes before slicing. This allows the pork to reach the final temperature of 145°F (63°C) while also ensuring that its natural juices make their way back to the center of the roast.

When the roast is cool enough to handle, cut off the twine and carve the roast into ½-inch (1.5 cm) slices. Shingle the pieces across a serving platter and drizzle with the "tonnato" sauce. Serve the pork with lemon wedges and the collected pan juices poured over the top.

SPANISH PICNIC

Picnics can be magical. Throw a blanket on the ground, crack open a cold beverage, unpack a snack, and enjoy time with friends or family outside. Whether you are escaping the hustle and bustle of New York City at the Bow Bridge in Central Park, enjoying Barcelona from high above the city at Bunkers del Carmel, or watching the boats drift down the Thames at London's Furnival Gardens, a few cans of tinned fish are sure to elevate your afternoon picnic spread.

Here are some guidelines to build out a satisfying (and portable) feast. Don't feel restrained by the list, though; follow your taste buds and sense of adventure to create your own magical afternoon.

A few different tins of fish: try mackerel, smoked oysters, and anchovies

Some cured meats: chorizo, morcilla, and jamón are among the best

A few containers of mixed olives

A selection of Spanish cheeses: Manchego, Cabrales, and Tetilla will give you a delicious variety

A tomato or two for slicing

A crusty baguette

A container of butter and flaky sea salt—always a good idea

A few cold beers (try a Spanish lager, such as Estrella Galicia) or a bottle of red wine (when you mix red wine with lemon soda, it becomes the delicious tinto de verano, a Spanish drink similar to sangria)

Whatever you decide to bring, just make sure you are surrounded by lovely people and warm vibes, and you can't go wrong.

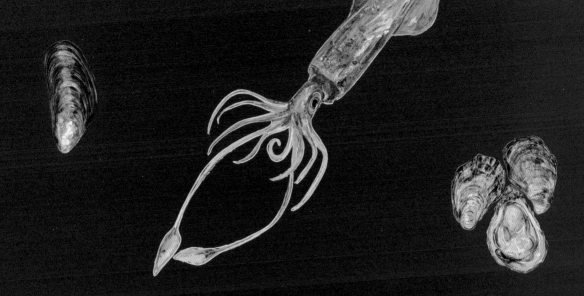

SHELLFISH, SQUID, AND OCTOPUS

CRUSTACEA AND *MOLLUSCA*

CRABS, CLAMS, MUSSELS, OYSTERS, SEA URCHIN, SQUID, and octopus all fall under the umbrella term of shellfish. There are three categories of shellfish: crustaceans, mollusks, and cephalopods. Although they have similar characteristics, there are some major differences.

Crustaceans, such as crabs, shrimp, lobster, and crayfish, are animals that have a jointed outer skeleton or shell that they shed as they grow. Aside from being widely consumed by humans, they play a major role in the aquatic food chain. They serve as sustenance for many marine predators, including fish and whales.

Mollusks are animals that have either one or two shells that expand as the animal grows. Examples of mollusks are clams, mussels, oysters, and scallops. Mollusks have played an important part in the history of humans, not just for food but also for tools and jewelry. In their natural habitat, the sea, mollusks are little water-filtration systems, cleaning the water as it passes through their shells in search of food.

Cephalopods are technically a type of mollusk. These animals have soft bodies but without the outer shell to protect them. Squid, octopus, and cuttlefish are all examples of cephalopods. All cephalopods have the ability to squirt ink, a technique they use to confuse predators.

Shellfish have been eaten around the world for centuries, and for good reason. Aside from being delicious, they are a very healthful form of protein to include in your diet. Tinned shellfish is a great source for omega-3s, zinc, iron, magnesium, and vitamin B_{12}. Shellfish are also a very lean protein and are extremely low in saturated fats. Having a balanced amount of shellfish in your diet can promote brain function and heart health. They help do things like lower the risk of heart disease, boost your immune system, and aid in weight loss.

In this chapter, you will learn how diverse and tasty tinned shellfish can be. You can use their brininess to make a delicious Spaghetti with Clams, White Wine, and Chili Flakes (page 137), their richness to create a crowd-pleasing Crab Mac and Cheese (page 128), and their texture for a play on the classic pulpo a la Gallega (Octopus with Crispy Potatoes and Aioli, page 163). As you cook your way through this chapter, keep an open mind. You may not be accustomed to seeing mussels or squid in tins, but I think you'll come to appreciate the taste and convenience of this long food tradition that was born in Spain.

WHAT'S IN THE TIN

Tinned shellfish come in many varieties, from the more recognizable clam to the less known octopus. They also come packed in many different flavors, such as smoked, in tomato sauce, pickled, or simply tinned in their own brine. Each recipe in this chapter will suggest a flavor profile for the recipe. If the recipe calls for the shellfish in brine, stick with it because not only does the brine add flavor, it is also used as a seasoning agent. Otherwise, feel free to mix and match tin flavors to put your own spin on the recipes.

A quick note on tinned crab: Good tinned crab is generally sold in 8-ounce (225 g) containers (and PS, it should always be picked through for bits of shells). This means you will usually have crab left over, as the recipes in this book call for less than 8 ounces (225 g). You can freeze any leftover crab in an airtight container or plastic bag for up to 3 months. If you like to plan ahead, I suggest weighing the crab for each future recipe you plan on cooking and then freezing it separately. Just make sure you label each bag with the amount so you don't forget later on.

CRAB HUSH PUPPIES WITH JALAPEÑO TARTAR SAUCE

Hush puppies are deep-fried cornmeal fritters that are a classic at fish fries in the American South. This recipe takes them up a notch with the addition of crabmeat but keeps them light and fluffy. Serve them with a jalapeño-spiked tartar sauce for dipping. These are a great addition to your next party spread.

===== MAKES 20 HUSH PUPPIES =====

JALAPEÑO TARTAR SAUCE

1 cup (225 g) mayonnaise

1 medium shallot, minced

2 jalapeños, seeded and minced

1 tablespoon capers, minced

2 tablespoons minced dill pickle

1 teaspoon pickle brine

1 teaspoon hot sauce

Juice of ½ lemon

CRAB HUSH PUPPIES

1 large egg

1 clove garlic, grated with a Microplane

½ cup plus 1 tablespoon (135 ml) buttermilk

2 tablespoons minced fresh chives

½ cup (75 g) cornmeal

¼ cup plus 2 tablespoons (45 g) all-purpose flour

½ teaspoon baking powder

1 teaspoon Old Bay Seasoning

½ teaspoon freshly ground black pepper

1 teaspoon kosher salt, plus more for sprinkling

½ cup (3 ounces/85 g) crabmeat, picked clean of bits of shell

Neutral oil, such as grapeseed or canola, for deep-frying

To make the jalapeño tartar sauce: In a medium bowl, combine the mayonnaise, shallot, jalapeños, capers, pickle, pickle brine, hot sauce, and lemon juice and stir well. If saving for later, transfer the mixture to a covered container and refrigerate for up to 1 week. If using in the next couple hours or so, leave the sauce covered on your counter. Nothing ruins a great fried snack like a cold dipping sauce.

To make the crab hush puppies: In a bowl, stir together the egg, garlic, buttermilk, and chives. In a second larger bowl, stir together the cornmeal, flour, baking powder, Old Bay, pepper, and salt. Gently stir the buttermilk mixture into the cornmeal mixture until fully incorporated. (Take care not to be too aggressive here. Overmixing makes for tough hush puppies.)

Continued

Gently fold in the crabmeat and allow the batter to rest for at least 10 minutes but no more than 30 minutes in the refrigerator.

While the batter is resting, pour 4 inches (10 cm) of neutral oil into a deep pot and heat to 365°F (185°C).

When the oil is up to temperature, working in batches, carefully drop the batter by the tablespoon into the oil and cook, turning occasionally, until golden brown, 2 to 3 minutes. Remove the cooked hush puppies to a plate lined with paper towels and sprinkle with salt. Depending on the size of the pot, it will probably take four or five batches to fry all the hush puppies.

Make sure you allow the hush puppies to rest for a minute or so before serving alongside the jalapeño tartar sauce.

BOMBOLOTTI WITH CRAB, BACON, AND CREAMED CORN

Sweet crab, smoky bacon, and creamy corn are a match made in heaven. Tossing them with stubby tube-shaped bombolotti pasta is a plus because the tubes fill with the delicious sauce. The bombolotti is about half the size of rigatoni and has ridges to catch the sauce, too. You can make this recipe with canned creamed corn or, if you have some extra time on your hands, try making the creamed corn yourself. The result will be a more flavorful and rewarding pasta.

SERVES 2

1 teaspoon olive oil

2 slices (50 g) bacon, cut crosswise into strips ½ inch (1.5 cm) wide

1 cup (210 g) creamed corn, homemade (recipe follows) or from one 8.25-ounce (235 g) can

Kosher salt

6.5 ounces (185 g) bombolotti or rigatoni pasta

6 ounces (170 g) crabmeat, picked clean of bits of shell

1 tablespoon unsalted butter

2 tablespoons grated Parmesan cheese

1 tablespoon minced fresh chives

5 large basil leaves, roughly chopped

Lemon, for squeezing

Freshly ground black pepper

Bring a large pot of water to a boil over high heat for the pasta. This can take up to 20 minutes, depending on your stove. Use this time to gather the rest of your ingredients.

In a large skillet, combine the olive oil and sliced bacon and cook over medium heat until the bacon fat is rendered and the bacon becomes crispy and delicious. Add the creamed corn, stir to combine, and remove from the heat.

Add enough salt to the boiling water so that it reminds you of a less salty sea. Add the pasta and cook according to the package directions, stirring the pasta every 2 minutes or so to ensure that it doesn't stick together. Taste a noodle a minute or so before the end of the suggested cooking time to ensure that your pasta comes out al dente.

Scoop out ¼ cup (60 ml) of pasta water, then drain the pasta and add it to the bacon-corn mixture. Set the pan over medium high, add the reserved pasta water along with the crabmeat, and start stirring and tossing the pasta with the sauce. After about 30 seconds, add the butter and stir to emulsify. Once the butter is emulsified, remove from the heat and stir in the Parmesan, chives, basil, and a squeeze of lemon juice.

Divide the pasta between two bowls and garnish with a few cracks of black pepper.

Creamed Corn

Creamed corn is best with fresh corn you grow yourself or buy from a local farmer. This recipe makes more than you need for the pasta. Use the leftovers as a dinner side dish; top it with chopped rosemary and Parmesan before bringing it to the table.

MAKES 2 CUPS (420 G)

4 ears corn, shucked

1 cup (240 ml) heavy cream

Kosher salt and freshly ground black pepper

Use your largest bowl as well as your smallest to make collecting the corn kernels easy and clean. Overturn the small bowl in the center of the larger one. Rest an ear of corn, pointy end up, against the small bowl. Using a serrated knife, carefully cut the kernels from the cob, allowing them to fall into the larger bowl. Repeat with the remaining ears. Set the kernels aside, and be sure to keep the cobs.

Holding a corncob over a large saucepot, use the back of a butter knife to scrape the cob to get as much "corn milk" out as possible. Repeat for all the cobs; the amount will vary from cob to cob, so don't worry if it isn't the same. Add the cobs and cream to the corn milk and bring to a boil over high heat. Immediately remove from the heat and rest for 10 minutes or so.

Strain the corn milk liquid through a fine-mesh sieve into another saucepot. Add the reserved kernels to the pot and bring to a rapid simmer over high heat. Reduce the heat to medium-low and cook until tender, about 12 minutes.

Season the mixture with salt and pepper. Transfer one-third of the mixture to a blender and process until smooth. Return the puree to the pot. Creamed corn can be used immediately or stored in an airtight container in the refrigerator for up to 3 days.

CRAB MAC AND CHEESE

Nothing says comfort food like mac and cheese, and adding tinned crab to the traditional roux-based cheese sauce takes the dish to a whole other level. This version is simple enough for a weeknight dinner but decadent enough for a dinner party. The Calabrian chile adds a bit of heat but can easily be omitted if spicy mac and cheese isn't your thing.

===== SERVES 6 =====

½ cup (40 g) panko bread crumbs

½ cup (50 g) grated Parmesan cheese

2 teaspoons olive oil

2 teaspoons fresh thyme

2 tablespoons unsalted butter

2 tablespoons all-purpose flour

Kosher salt

½ teaspoon freshly ground black pepper

3 tablespoons chopped Calabrian chile

3½ cups (840 ml) whole milk, warmed

1 cup (115 g) shredded Cheddar cheese

10 ounces (285 g) crabmeat, picked clean of bits of shell

12 ounces (340 g) cavatappi pasta (fusilli would make a great substitute)

2 scallions, thinly sliced

Bring a large pot of water to a boil over high heat for the pasta. This can take up to 20 minutes, depending on your stove. Use this time to gather the rest of your ingredients.

In a small bowl, mix together the panko, Parmesan, olive oil, and thyme. Set aside.

In a large saucepot, melt the butter over medium heat. Add the flour, 1 teaspoon salt, and the pepper and whisk constantly until the mixture is bubbling and light tan. This should take only a minute or two. Add the chile and stir to incorporate. What you are making here is called a roux. Used traditionally in French kitchens to thicken everything from sauces to gravies, it is an indispensable tool for any home cook.

Add the warmed milk in a slow but steady stream to the roux and whisk until the sauce begins to thicken, 4 to 5 minutes. Reduce the heat to low, add the Cheddar, and whisk until the cheese is melted and the sauce is smooth. Add the crab and remove from the heat.

Add enough salt to the boiling water so that it reminds you of a less salty sea. Add the pasta and cook according to the package directions, stirring the pasta every 2 minutes or so to ensure that it doesn't stick together. Taste a noodle a minute or so before the end of the suggested cooking time to ensure that your pasta comes out al dente. Drain the pasta.

Preheat the broiler.

Add the drained pasta to the cheese sauce and stir over low heat until all the pasta is coated and everything is warmed through. Pour the pasta mixture into an 8-inch (20 cm) square broilerproof baking dish or one of similar size, taking care to use a silicone spatula to scrape all the sauce from the pot. Use the spatula to spread the mac and cheese in an even layer.

Sprinkle the panko mixture across the top of the mac and cheese, place under the broiler, and broil until browned, about 1 minute. Remove from the broiler and garnish with sliced scallions.

CRAB, BACON, EGG, AND CHEESE ON A ROLL

The deli classic of bacon, egg, and cheese on a roll gets an update with sweet crabmeat and a salty and crusty kaiser or pretzel roll. American cheese is the obvious choice for an egg sandwich because of its melting capabilities, but you could use thinly sliced Cheddar. If you have homemade aioli, try it here, but store-bought mayo works well, too.

MAKES 2 SANDWICHES

2 slices smoked bacon, each cut into thirds

2 kaiser or pretzel rolls

2½ tablespoons unsalted butter

3½ ounces (100 g) crabmeat, picked clean of bits of shell

2 large eggs, whisked

Kosher salt

2 slices American cheese

Mayonnaise or Aioli (page 164)

In a nonstick pan, cook the bacon over medium heat until crispy, 2 to 3 minutes per side. Transfer to a paper towel, keeping the rendered fat in the pan.

Slice the rolls in half horizontally. Add 2 tablespoons of the butter to the bacon fat and cook until it begins to bubble. Add the rolls cut side down and cook until golden and crispy, about 2 minutes. Transfer the rolls to the plates they will eventually be served on.

Wipe the pan clean, add the remaining ½ tablespoon butter, and bring to a bubble over medium-high heat. Add the crabmeat in a single layer and cook, undisturbed, until the crab is starting to brown, about 3 minutes. Give the crab a quick stir before adding the eggs. Scramble the eggs to the consistency you prefer, about 2 minutes for a medium scramble. Season with salt.

Divide the eggs between the two bottom halves of the toasted rolls. Place a slice of American cheese on top of the eggs, followed by the bacon slices, add a generous smear of mayo or aioli to each of the top buns, and put the buns back together. Boom! CBEC.

RAZOR CLAM BRUSCHETTA WITH CALABRIAN CHILE BUTTER AND HERBS

Razor clams are the long, narrow clams that are found in saltwater. They're supersweet and tender, and the brine of tinned razor clams along with bright herbs is a great contrast to the charred bread and rich butter in this bruschetta. You'll want to make sure you keep the butter cold up to the point you put it on the bread. The texture it adds allows each bite to taste a bit different. Eat bruschetta as a light lunch or as an appetizer at the dinner table.

==================== MAKES 2 TOASTS ====================

CALABRIAN CHILE BUTTER

1 stick (4 ounces/115 g) unsalted butter, at room temperature

1 tablespoon chopped Calabrian chile

Grated zest and juice of ½ lemon

BRUSCHETTA

One 4-ounce (115 g) tin razor clams in brine, brine reserved

Olive oil

Juice of ½ lemon

2 slices country sourdough bread, about 1 inch (2.5 cm) thick

10 chives, cut into 1-inch (2.5 cm) lengths

5 large mint leaves, torn into small pieces

Small handful of fresh parsley

¼ bulb fennel, thinly shaved

Kosher salt and freshly ground black pepper

To make the Calabrian chile butter: In a food processor, blend the butter until smooth, scraping the sides of the bowl a few times with a silicone spatula to ensure that all the butter gets softened. Add the chile and blend until it is fully incorporated. Scrape the sides again, but don't worry if a few chunks of chile remain. Add the lemon zest and lemon juice and blend until incorporated. Transfer the butter to a covered container and refrigerate until the butter hardens, about 1 hour.

To prepare the bruschetta: Remove the clams from the tin, taking care to reserve the brine. Slice the clams into thumbnail-size pieces. (When the clams are cleaned, they are separated into the digger foot and siphon. The siphon looks a bit strange, but trust me, it's delicious, so make sure nothing is left behind.)

Place the clam pieces in a small bowl. Add 1 teaspoon of the reserved clam brine, 1 teaspoon olive oil, and the lemon juice. Toss and set aside to marinate while you make the toasts.

Heat a cast-iron skillet over medium-high heat. Drizzle both sides of the bread with some olive oil. Cook the bread in the pan until both sides are charred and crispy but the inside is still slightly chewy; 2 to 3 minutes per side should do the trick. (You can also do this under the oven's broiler if need be.)

Immediately top the warm toast with "peels" of the Calabrian chile butter: Do this by scraping the top of the butter toward you with a small spoon to get pieces a couple inches (5 cm) long. Make sure you cover one side of the toast completely with the butter, without too much overlap.

Add the chives, mint, parsley, and fennel to the clams and toss to coat everything with the liquid. Season with salt and pepper.

Divide the razor clam salad between the two pieces of buttered toast. Cut each piece in half, if you prefer, and enjoy.

CLAM DIP

Tinned clams combined with cream cheese, sour cream, and hot sauce makes for a no-cook clam dip that comes together in minutes and is always a crowd favorite. For best results, allow the dip to rest in your refrigerator for a few hours before serving. Potato chips are a great accompaniment.

===== MAKES 2 CUPS (410 g) =====

¼ cup (65 g) cream cheese, at room temperature

¾ cup (180 g) sour cream

1 teaspoon hot sauce

¾ teaspoon Worcestershire sauce

Two 6.5-ounce (185 g) tins whole clams (see Note)

2 tablespoons minced fresh chives

Juice of ¼ lemon

Pinch of cayenne pepper

Sturdy potato chips, for serving

In a food processor, blend the cream cheese until smooth. Add the sour cream, hot sauce, and Worcestershire sauce and pulse until incorporated. Add the clams, 1 tablespoon of the chives, the lemon juice, and cayenne. Pulse until just incorporated. The dip is more delicious if it has small pieces of clams instead of clam puree, so be sure not to overpulse.

Transfer the clam dip to a serving bowl and garnish with the remaining 1 tablespoon chives. Enjoy with your favorite crunchy potato chips.

NOTE: If chopped clams are all you can find at your local grocer, don't fret. Simply fold them into the dip using a silicone spatula after everything else has been incorporated.

SPAGHETTI WITH CLAMS, WHITE WINE, AND CHILI FLAKES

Spaghetti alle vongole (spaghetti with clams), a classic Italian pasta dish that comes from the city of Naples, could arguably be the best pasta dish of all time. There are vongole recipes that will tell you to add tomatoes, butter, or even mushrooms to the dish, but pasta with clams is best when kept simple: briny, a bit spicy, and undeniably delicious. You won't skip a beat subbing high-quality tinned clams for fresh ones.

SERVES 2

2 tablespoons olive oil

2 cloves garlic, smashed

Small pinch of chili flakes

¼ cup (60 ml) dry white wine

One 4-ounce (115 g) tin whole clams in brine

2 tablespoons chopped fresh parsley

Kosher salt

6 ounces (170 g) spaghetti

Bring a large pot of water to a boil over high heat for the pasta. This can take up to 20 minutes, depending on your stove. Use this time to gather the rest of your ingredients.

In a large skillet, combine the olive oil and garlic and set the pan over medium heat. The idea here is to slowly toast the garlic, which will in turn infuse the oil. After 2 minutes or so of flipping the garlic a few times, you should end up with golden cloves. (If you turn your head and the garlic burns, do yourself a favor and toss the oil and garlic and start over. Burnt garlic = bitter oil.)

Remove the pan from the heat and add the chili flakes, followed immediately by the wine. Add the brine from the tinned clams and half of the parsley. Return the pan to the heat and cook until reduced by half.

Add enough salt to the boiling water so that it tastes like a slightly salted glass of water. You don't want to season the pasta water

too aggressively here because the brine of the clams is a bit salty already. Add the spaghetti and cook according to the package directions, stirring the pasta every 2 minutes or so to ensure that it doesn't stick together. Taste a noodle a minute or so before the end of the suggested cooking time to ensure that your pasta comes out al dente.

Reserve ¼ cup (60 ml) of the pasta cooking water, drain the pasta, and add the water and pasta to the pan along with the clams. Cook over medium-high heat, flipping and tossing along the way, until you have reduced most of the liquid and the bottom of the pan looks glossy. This will take only a minute, so keep a close eye.

Add the remaining parsley and give the pasta one final toss. Divide it between two bowls and enjoy.

MUSSEL SALAD WITH FENNEL, CHICKPEAS, AND DILL VINAIGRETTE

Mussels cooked with chickpeas are a staple in kitchens across many countries. There is something magical about the contrast between the nutty and creamy chickpeas and the plump and briny mussels. This recipe builds on the tradition but incorporates the ingredients into a refreshing salad brightened by a dill vinaigrette.

SERVES 2

DILL VINAIGRETTE

½ teaspoon Dijon mustard

2 tablespoons chopped fresh dill

3 tablespoons olive oil

Grated zest and juice of ½ lemon

1 clove garlic, peeled

Fish sauce

MUSSEL SALAD

1 medium bulb fennel, halved through the root end

2 red radishes

One 15-ounce (425 g) can chickpeas, drained and rinsed

1 tablespoon chopped capers

One 4.2-ounce (120 g) tin smoked mussels in broth

Small handful of arugula, for garnish

To make the vinaigrette: In a small bowl, stir together the mustard, dill, olive oil, lemon zest, and lemon juice. This is a "broken" vinaigrette, so don't worry if it doesn't look emulsified. Add the garlic by grating it over the bowl with a Microplane. Season with fish sauce to taste and set aside. If you're not using this immediately, it will hold in an airtight container, refrigerated, for 3 days.

To prepare the mussel salad: Working over a large bowl and using a mandoline, thinly shave the fennel starting at the bottom of the bulb and working your way toward the fronds. Repeat the process with the radishes.

Add the chickpeas to the bowl and toss to combine. Add the capers and stir to combine.

Continued

Taste the broth of the tinned mussels; if you think it's delicious, add it, along with the mussels, to the bowl. If not, drain the mussels before adding them to the bowl. Gently stir to combine, taking care to keep the mussels as intact as possible.

Add the dill vinaigrette to the mussel salad and gently stir, coating the chickpeas and vegetables.

Spoon the salad into serving bowls and garnish with a couple pieces of arugula.

MUSSEL SALAD AND POTATO CHIPS ON A BRIOCHE BUN

Thanks to tinned mussels, this salad keeps well, which means it's great to have in your refrigerator at all times to make a quick snack with crackers or a delicious lunch when piled onto a brioche bun. Adding potato chips atop the salad gives a salty crunch to the sandwich. When you're mixing the salad, use a gentle touch; do your best to not turn the mussels to mush. The salad will keep for 3 or 4 days before the flavors start to muddy; the sandwich should be eaten as soon as it is assembled.

MAKES 2 SANDWICHES

MUSSEL SALAD

¼ cup (55 g) mayonnaise

1 tablespoon chopped fresh tarragon

1 tablespoon chopped fresh parsley

1 stalk celery, thinly sliced

2 scallions, thinly sliced

Juice of ½ lemon

One 4-ounce (115 g) tin mussels in oil and vinegar

SANDWICHES

2 brioche hot dog buns

Small handful of potato chips, preferably Lay's Original, plus more for serving

Small pinch of Old Bay Seasoning

To make the mussel salad: In a medium bowl, combine the mayonnaise, tarragon, parsley, celery, scallions, and lemon juice. Using a silicone spatula, fold the ingredients until you have a cohesive dressing of sorts. Gently fold in the mussels, taking care not to mash them or turn them into mush.

To assemble the sandwiches: Divide the mussel salad equally between the brioche buns. Using your hands, crush a small amount of potato chips over the salad. Sprinkle with the Old Bay and serve more potato chips alongside.

TURKISH FRIED MUSSELS AND TARATOR ON A HOAGIE ROLL

What makes these Turkish street sandwiches delicious, aside from the crispy mussels, is the creamy tarator sauce made from walnuts, garlic, and bread crumbs. To ensure that your batter sticks to the mussels when frying, make sure they are whole and blotted dry with a paper towel before dipping them in the batter and placing in the oil.

MAKES 2 SANDWICHES

½ cup (65 g) all-purpose flour

¾ cup (175 ml) cold lager beer

1 egg yolk, beaten

⅓ cup (35 g) walnuts

⅓ cup (15 g) fresh bread crumbs

1 clove garlic, minced

1½ tablespoons red wine vinegar

¼ cup (60 ml) olive oil

Kosher salt

Neutral oil, such as grapeseed or canola

Two 4-ounce (115 g) tins mussels in vinegar, carefully removed from the tins and blotted dry

2 hoagie rolls (you could use hot dog rolls in a pinch)

¼ red onion, thinly sliced

Small handful of mixed fresh parsley and mint

Hefty pinch of sumac or grated lemon zest

Lemon, for squeezing

Place the flour in a medium bowl. Slowly whisk the beer into the flour, followed by the egg yolk. Place the bowl in the refrigerator while you prep the rest of your ingredients.

In a blender or food processor, combine the walnuts and bread crumbs. Pulse them a few times so that they become a crumble with pieces the size of peas. Add the garlic and pulse again. Add the vinegar and puree until smooth. (Add a splash of water if you need a little help to get things moving.) With the blender on, slowly drizzle in the olive oil until you have an emulsified sauce. Taste and season with salt. Set the tarator sauce aside.

Pour 2 inches (5 cm) of grapeseed or canola oil into a medium heavy-bottomed pot and warm over medium-high heat until it reaches 350°F (180°C). Line a plate with a few paper towels. This is where the mussels will land once they come out of the oil.

Remove the beer batter from the refrigerator and carefully place the mussels in the batter. Gently submerge the mussels to ensure that they are completely coated in the batter. Working in batches if needed to avoid crowding, remove the mussels one at time from the batter, shaking off any excess, and carefully place in the hot oil. Fry the mussels for 2 minutes. Transfer the fried mussels to the prepared plate and season with salt.

Once all the mussels are fried, divide them between the hoagie rolls. Add the onion, herbs, and sumac to each sandwich. Drizzle with as much tarator sauce as you'd like, and squeeze a bit of lemon juice over the top. Share the sandwiches with a friend or keep them both for yourself.

SMOKED OYSTER SPREAD

Be warned: This smoked oyster spread is highly addictive! Smoky, creamy, and with just the right amount of spice, this quick-to-make snack is an obvious choice for game day or a barbecue.

MAKES 3 TO 4 CUPS (ABOUT 900 g)

16 ounces (455 g) cream cheese, at room temperature

1 cup (225 g) mayonnaise

1 tablespoon prepared horseradish

1 shallot, grated on the small holes of a box grater

2 cloves garlic, grated on the small holes of a box grater

2 tablespoons chopped fresh parsley

1 tablespoon Old Bay Seasoning

1 tablespoon Dijon mustard

1 teaspoon hot sauce

Grated zest and juice of ½ lemon

Two 3-ounce (85 g) tins smoked oysters, drained

1 scallion, thinly sliced

4 slices bacon, cooked until crisped and crumbled

Saltines, for serving

In a food processor, combine the cream cheese, mayonnaise, horseradish, shallot, garlic, parsley, Old Bay, mustard, hot sauce, lemon zest, and lemon juice. Blend until smooth, taking care to scrape down the sides of the bowl a few times to ensure that everything gets incorporated.

Add the drained oysters and give the processor a few quick pulses to incorporate everything.

Transfer the spread to a serving bowl and garnish with the scallion and crumbled bacon. Serve with saltines.

SMOKED OYSTERS, SALTINES, AND HOT SAUCE

This is less a recipe than it is a lesson in how three humble things can add up to be so much more than the sum of their parts. I've eaten this snack on just about every fishing trip I've been on. It's also a portable feast to take with you on a hike through the woods. A cold beer goes down easily alongside.

SERVES 1

1 tin smoked oysters

1 small sleeve saltines

1 small bottle or a few packets of your favorite hot sauce

Pull an oyster from the tin, place it on a cracker, and apply a few dashes of hot sauce. Repeat until all the oysters are eaten.

SPAGHETTI WITH SMOKED OYSTERS AND EGG YOLKS

Spaghetti alla carbonara is one of the classic pasta dishes from the Eternal City of Rome. It is typically cooked with guanciale (cured pork jowl) to get a salty-smoky flavor; here you'll use tinned smoked oysters for the same effect. And use the freshest eggs you can find. The result is a bowl of creamy and satisfying umami-filled pasta.

SERVES 2

Kosher salt

6 ounces (170 g) spaghetti

2 teaspoons olive oil

½ teaspoon freshly cracked black pepper

One 3-ounce (85 g) tin smoked oysters in oil

3 tablespoons grated pecorino cheese

2 egg yolks, beaten

1½ tablespoons minced fresh chives

Bring a large pot of water to a boil over high heat for the pasta. This can take up to 20 minutes, depending on your stove. Use this time to gather the rest of your ingredients.

Add enough salt to the boiling water so that it reminds you of a less salty sea. Add the pasta and cook according to the package directions, stirring the pasta every 2 minutes or so to ensure that it doesn't stick together. Taste a noodle a minute or so before the end of the suggested cooking time to ensure that your pasta comes out al dente.

While the pasta is cooking, in a skillet, warm the olive oil and black pepper over medium heat. As soon as you can smell the pepper, remove the pan from the heat and allow to cool for a minute or so before adding ⅓ cup (80 ml) of the boiling pasta water. Add the smoked oysters and their oil.

Scoop the pasta out of the water with a skimmer or strainer and add to the pan. (Anytime you are cooking pasta it is always a good idea to retain the pasta cooking water in case you need a bit of it to thin the sauce out later.) Set the pan over medium-high heat and toss and stir the pasta until there is very little liquid left in the pan. Remove from the heat and add the pecorino. Flip and stir until the cheese is one with the pasta.

This next step will make or break your carbonara. It is important to work quickly, but not too quickly, and to make sure the noodles are hot enough to slowly cook the egg but not so hot that they scramble.

With a silicone spatula in hand, pour the egg yolks over the pasta. Quickly work the eggs through the pasta by stirring it evenly around the pan with your spatula. Use the spatula to keep the yolks from sitting on the bottom of the pan for more than a second or two while you are tossing the pasta. Once the eggs are creamy, warm, and thickened, you're ready to serve the pasta. Divide it between two bowls and sprinkle with the chives.

MALFALDINE WITH SHISHITO PEPPERS AND SEA URCHIN

Sea urchin, or uni as it is known in Japan, is a delicacy eaten in many countries. Because of its subtle flavor, it is best enjoyed with things that are more neutral, such as pasta. Tinned sea urchin is pricier than most tinned fish but is worth the splurge when you want to treat yourself. Make sure to add the uni just before you're ready to eat to avoid cooking it further.

SERVES 4

2 tablespoons olive oil

2 tablespoons minced shallot

½ cup (35 g) thinly sliced shishito pepper rings

½ cup (120 ml) white wine

½ cup (120 ml) heavy cream

Kosher salt

12 ounces (340 g) malfaldine pasta or other strand pasta

2 tablespoons unsalted butter

One 4-ounce (115 g) tin sea urchin

3 tablespoons chopped fresh parsley

Lemon, for squeezing

Bring a large pot of water to a boil over high heat for the pasta. This can take up to 20 minutes, depending on your stove. Use this time to gather the rest of your ingredients.

In a large skillet or rondeau, heat the olive oil and shallot over medium heat. Cook the shallot until it is soft but does not take on any color, about 2 minutes. Add the shishito peppers and cook for another minute. You are simply trying to bring out the sweetness and flavor of the peppers, so don't worry when they still seem a little crunchy; they will soften during the rest of the sauce-building process.

Increase the heat to high and immediately add the wine. Let it bubble and reduce by three-quarters, then add the cream. Reduce the cream mixture by half, but take care not to let it burn on the bottom of the pan. Keep things moving from the bottom up by stirring and sliding a silicone spatula across the bottom of the pan. Remove from the heat.

Add enough salt to the boiling water so that it reminds you of a less salty sea. Add the pasta and cook according to the package directions, stirring the pasta every 2 minutes or so to ensure that it doesn't stick together. Taste a noodle a minute or so before the end of the suggested cooking time to ensure that your pasta comes out al dente.

Reserving ¼ cup (60 ml) of the pasta cooking water, drain the pasta and add it and the reserved cooking water to the pan. Stir the pasta constantly over medium-high heat so it is evenly coated, then add the butter and give everything another stir.

Remove the pan from the heat. Stir in the sea urchin and continue stirring with the goal of gently breaking up the sea urchin but not breaking the noodles. Add the parsley and squeeze in some lemon juice. Try the pasta to make sure you can taste the lemon. If you can't, give it another squeeze.

Divide the pasta among four bowls and enjoy with a crisp white wine.

SQUID WITH CABBAGE, PEACH, HERBS, AND PEANUTS

Cool, crunchy, spicy, and herbaceous all come together in this fresh salad inspired by Thai flavors. Opt for baby squid in olive oil for this recipe; its canned cousin that is often stuffed or stored in ragu will throw off the balance of flavors here. If you aren't familiar with fish sauce, don't be put off by the pungent smell; the taste is much more relaxed than you'd think, and it adds a delicious and crucial element to this dish.

=========== SERVES 2 ===========

2 cups (140 g) shredded cabbage (I used Savoy, but any cabbage will work)

1½ tablespoons fish sauce

½ teaspoon sugar

1 Fresno chile, sliced into thin rings

1 serrano chile, sliced into thin rings

2 scallions, cut into ½-inch (1.5 cm) lengths

½ cup (75g) salted roasted peanuts, halved

1 peach, thinly sliced

Two 3.8-ounce (110 g) tins baby squid

½ cup (15 g) fresh cilantro

½ cup (15 g) fresh mint

Juice of 3 limes

In a large bowl, combine the cabbage, fish sauce, and sugar and gently massage the cabbage with your hands for 20 seconds or so before allowing it to rest for 5 minutes. This helps soften the cabbage just slightly and ensures that all the cabbage is evenly coated.

Add both chiles, the scallions, half of the peanuts, the peach slices, and baby squid to the bowl and fold gently with a wooden spoon or silicone spatula. Fold in the cilantro and mint. Add the lime juice and fold again.

Divide the salad between two bowls and sprinkle with the remaining peanuts before serving.

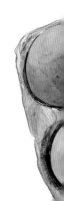

GRILLED EGGPLANT OMELET WITH SQUID IN RAGU AND CELERY

Grilled eggplant has a wonderfully smoky flavor and custardy texture and is a welcome addition to this Filipino-style omelet. The squid in ragu has an intense peppery flavor and brininess. An eggplant omelet makes a wonderful breakfast or light lunch on its own, but if you're a bit hungrier, serve it alongside a bowl of steamed rice.

SERVES 2

2 Japanese eggplants

2 tablespoons neutral oil, plus a bit for brushing the eggplant

Kosher salt and freshly ground black pepper

2 large eggs

Two 4-ounce (120 g) tins squid in ragu

½ cup (15 g) celery leaves (use the inner yellow leaves)

Lemon, for squeezing

Heat a grill to medium-high. (If grilling is not an option, you can always use the broiler in your oven.)

Using a fork, gently poke several holes in each eggplant. This will help with even cooking, but it also makes the skin easier to peel later on. Lightly brush the eggplant with neutral oil and place on the grill. Cook each eggplant until all the skin is charred and the eggplant is soft to the touch, about 6 minutes, but turn the eggplants every 2 minutes or so. Transfer the eggplants to a plate and cover with a kitchen towel until they're cool enough to handle. Covering the eggplants with a towel helps to steam the skin loose.

With the eggplants still lying on the plate, peel them starting at the top (the stem end) and working your way to the bottom. Keep the stem on to keep the eggplant intact. This will make cooking them easier.

Using the back of your fork, gently press the eggplants flat. Season them lightly with salt and pepper.

Continued

Crack the eggs into a large bowl. Season the eggs lightly with salt and pepper and whisk with a fork. Add the eggplant and submerge. If your bowl can't fit both eggplants comfortably, do one at a time.

Heat a large nonstick or cast-iron skillet over medium heat. When it's hot, add the 2 tablespoons oil. With the bowl full of eggs and eggplant close to the stove, carefully slide the eggplants with the eggs into the pan. (Again, if your pan isn't large enough for both eggplants to fit comfortably, just work with one at a time.) Cook until both sides are golden brown, about 6 minutes, flipping them halfway through. With a slotted spatula, transfer the omelets to a plate lined with paper towels.

Put each omelet on a plate. Remove the squid from the tins and scatter them over the omelets. Scatter on the celery leaves and drizzle the remaining ragu from the tins on top of the omelets. Finish by squeezing a little fresh lemon juice on top. Eat immediately.

CALAMARATA WITH SQUID IN ITS OWN INK

Calamarata is a pasta shape that resembles the body of a squid that has been cut into rings. The pasta comes from the seaside towns around Naples, where it often gets paired with seafood-based sauces. Squid ink adds a rich and briny flavor to your pasta without being overpowering. It also gives the pasta a dark, inky color.

===== SERVES 2 =====

2 tablespoons olive oil

2 cloves garlic, thinly sliced

¼ teaspoon chili flakes

¼ cup (60 ml) white wine

One 4-ounce (115 g) tin squid in ink

Kosher salt

6 ounces (170 g) calamarata pasta or other short tube pasta such as bombolotti

3 tablespoons unsalted butter

2 tablespoons minced fresh chives

Lemon, for squeezing

Bring a large pot of water to a boil over high heat for the pasta. This can take up to 20 minutes, depending on your stove. Use this time to gather the rest of your ingredients.

In a skillet, heat the olive oil and garlic over medium heat and cook until the garlic is soft and fragrant, about 1 minute. Add the chili flakes immediately followed by the wine. Cook until the wine is reduced by half. Remove from the heat. Add the tinned squid and all of its ink to the garlic and wine mixture.

Add enough salt to the boiling water so that it reminds you of a less salty sea. Add the pasta and cook according to the package directions, stirring the pasta every 2 minutes or so to ensure that it doesn't stick together. Taste a noodle a minute or so before the end of the suggested cooking time to ensure that your pasta comes out al dente.

Reserving ¼ cup (60 ml) of the pasta cooking water, drain the pasta and add to the pan along with the reserved pasta water. Return to medium-high heat and cook the pasta until the sauce is reduced by half while tossing and stirring along the way. This will take 1 to 2 minutes.

Reduce the heat to low and add the butter. Constantly stir until the butter is completely melted and emulsified, 1 to 2 minutes. Stir in the chives and a squeeze of lemon juice.

Divide the pasta between two bowls and serve.

CALAMARI AND FARRO–STUFFED PEPPERS WITH SOUR CREAM

Calamari from Portugal is some of the best in the world, and José Gourmet does a delicious job of tinning some of the best on the market. Here it is used as a stuffing for flavorful red peppers. The recipe calls for farro, but any grain, such as rice or barley, will work.

MAKES 4 STUFFED PEPPERS

3 tablespoons unsalted butter

2 cloves garlic, minced

¼ cup (35 g) diced yellow onion

¼ cup (35 g) diced carrot

¼ cup (25 g) diced celery

¼ cup (40 g) golden raisins

1 teaspoon minced fresh rosemary

2 teaspoons minced fresh oregano

1 cup (195 g) farro, rinsed

1½ cups (360 ml) water

1 cup (240 ml) tomato juice

Kosher salt

Two 4.2-ounce (120 g) tins calamari in ragu

¼ cup (60 g) sour cream, plus more for serving

2 medium red bell peppers, halved lengthwise (through the stem) and seeded

Lemon, for squeezing

In a medium pot, heat the butter and garlic over medium heat and cook until the garlic becomes fragrant but doesn't get color. Add the onion and cook for 2 minutes. Add the carrot and celery and cook for 5 minutes. Add the raisins, rosemary, and oregano and cook for 1 minute. Add the farro and stir. Add the water and tomato juice and bring to a simmer over medium heat. Cook, uncovered, until the farro is fluffy and the liquid has been absorbed, about 25 minutes.

Season the farro mixture with salt. Pour onto a sheet pan or large dish and allow to cool at room temperature.

Meanwhile, preheat the oven to 375°F (190°C). Line a sheet pan with parchment paper.

Remove the calamari from the tins and pour any ragu left in the tins onto the farro. Slice the squid into ¼-inch (5 mm) rings. Stir the calamari and sour cream into the farro. Taste and season with salt if necessary.

Continued

Fill each half pepper with the farro mixture. You want the farro to sit just slightly above the edge of the pepper. Put the filled peppers on the prepared sheet pan and bake until they are soft but still have enough structure that they don't collapse under the weight of the farro, about 25 minutes.

Squeeze a little bit of lemon juice over each pepper. Dollop a small spoonful of sour cream over the peppers and serve immediately.

LULAS

RECHEADAS
EM MOLHO
MEDITERRÂNICO

Luças
Brand
SINCE 1896

LUÇAS & Cª Lᴰᴬ
MATOSINHOS · PORTUGAL

NET WT
115g [4,06z]

OCTOPUS WITH CRISPY POTATOES AND AIOLI

This is a play on the traditional pulpo a la Gallega, or Galician-style octopus. With its composed layers of meaty octopus, crispy potatoes, and creamy aioli, it's no wonder that this tapa is served at parties all across Spain. A generous sprinkle of smoked paprika and a drizzle of extra-virgin olive oil make the dish spicy, smoky, and floral.

SERVES 2 AS AN APPETIZER

11 ounces (310 g) small fingerling potatoes, scrubbed

1 bay leaf

4 cloves garlic, smashed

Kosher salt

Olive oil

Two 4-ounce (115 g) tins octopus in olive oil, drained and dried between two paper towels

2 teaspoons sherry vinegar

¼ cup (48 g) Aioli (recipe follows)

Pinch of smoked paprika or regular paprika

In a medium pot, combine the potatoes, bay leaf, garlic, and enough water to cover the potatoes by 2 inches (5 cm). Season with salt so that it reminds you of a slightly salty broth. Bring the pot to a gentle simmer and cook until the potatoes are just a little soft when you squeeze them between your fingers, about 15 minutes. Drain and let them dry on a kitchen towel.

When the potatoes are cool enough to handle, use the palm of your hand to carefully flatten them. They will not all look the same, and some will be more smooshed than others. This is a good thing. Once the potatoes are crisped, they will have varying degrees of nooks and crannies.

Have a slotted spoon and a bowl at the ready. In a skillet, heat a thin layer of olive oil over medium-high heat until hot but just before its smoke point. Carefully add the potatoes and cook until golden and crispy, about 2 minutes on each side. Remove the pan from the heat and use the slotted spoon to transfer the potatoes to the bowl.

Return the pan and oil to the heat and add the octopus, stirring until it begins to get a little color and some crispiness of its own. Be careful; the oil will spit a bit, so make sure you are using a kitchen towel to hold the pan. After a minute or two of the octopus dancing in the pan, transfer it to the bowl with the potatoes. Add the vinegar and a pinch of salt. Toss a few times, making sure most of the vinegar has been absorbed by the potatoes and octopus.

In the center of each of two serving plates, spread about 1 tablespoon of the aioli with the back of a spoon. Lay a few potatoes on each plate, followed by a bit more aioli, then some octopus. Repeat this process until all the potatoes and octopus are on the plates. Sprinkle with a generous pinch of paprika.

Aioli

The aioli will keep for at least 2 days in your refrigerator. And you can use it anywhere you use mayonnaise. Try it on the Crab, Bacon, Egg, and Cheese on a Roll (page 131).

MAKES 1 CUP (190 g)

2 egg yolks

4 cloves garlic, grated on a Microplane

½ cup (120 ml) olive oil

¼ cup (60 ml) neutral oil

Juice of 1 lemon

Kosher salt

Place the egg yolks in a medium bowl. Stir in the garlic and allow to rest for 5 minutes.

When making the aioli, you want to get all the oil into the egg yolks without the sauce breaking, so my little trick is to start small, by adding only 1 teaspoon of the olive oil at a time while constantly whisking. After 4 or 5 teaspoons, keep whisking while slowly pouring in a steady stream of olive oil until it is all emulsified. Repeat the steady stream with the neutral oil. Whisk in the lemon juice and season with salt.

matiz
ESPAÑA

PULPO
OCTOPUS
IN SPANISH OLIVE OIL

GOURMET

Conservas de Cambados

OCTOPUS
IN OLIVE OIL

NATURAL PRODUCT
WITHOUT PRESERVATIVES
OR ADDITIVES

Easy
open

ES
12.01/066/PO
CE.

gluten free

Ingredients: Octopus (Octopus vulgaris), olive oil and salt.
NET WEIGHT 4 OZ (111g)

Made in Spain by CONSERVAS DE CAMBADOS, S.L. FDA 15066
Barrantes - Ribadumia - Pontevedra (Spain)   Telf.: 0034 986 745 405

CELERY AND OCTOPUS SALAD WITH MEYER LEMON

In-season celery and octopus combine to make a salad that is super simple, super bright, and super delicious. Make sure to use your best extra-virgin olive oil and good tinned octopus like the one from Ramón Peña; and only farmers' market fresh celery will do.

SERVES 2

4 stalks celery, peeled and thinly sliced on the diagonal

¼ red onion, thinly sliced

2 cloves garlic, grated on a Microplane

½ teaspoon chili flakes

2 tablespoons extra-virgin olive oil

Grated zest and juice of 1 Meyer lemon

Two 4-ounce (115 g) tins octopus, drained

20 small sprigs parsley

20 celery leaves, from the inner and tender stalks

Kosher salt and freshly ground black pepper

In a medium bowl, combine the celery, onion, garlic, chili flakes, olive oil, and Meyer lemon zest and juice. Toss to coat and allow to rest for 5 minutes.

Add the octopus, parsley, and celery leaves to the bowl and toss to coat. Season with salt and pepper.

Divide the salad between two plates and enjoy.

OCTOPUS TOSTADA WITH ROASTED PINEAPPLE AND AVOCADO

Making tostadas is a great way to use slightly stale tortillas so that you don't have to toss them in the trash. It's the same concept as day-old bread making good toast. Top the tortillas with hearty black beans, rich avocado, and sweet and acidic pineapple, which work perfectly with the brininess of the octopus. When pan-roasting the pineapple, use a flat spatula to gently press the fruit to ensure that it gets evenly seared on both sides.

MAKES 4 TOSTADAS

4 tablespoons (60 ml) neutral oil

Three ¼-inch (5 mm) rings pineapple, cut from a peeled (but not cored) fresh pineapple

4 taco-size flour tortillas

1 cup (235 g) canned black beans, drained and rinsed

Kosher salt

¼ cup (20 g) thinly sliced red onion

1 tablespoon thinly sliced jalapeño rings

One 4-ounce (115 g) tin octopus in olive oil, drained

Lime, for squeezing

½ avocado, cut lengthwise into 8 slices

¼ cup (7 g) fresh cilantro

In a skillet, heat 1 tablespoon of the neutral oil over medium-high heat. Pat each slice of pineapple dry with a paper towel. When the oil in the skillet just begins to smoke, carefully lay down the pineapple rings and give a little shake so that they don't stick to the pan. Cook until the pineapple is slightly charred, about 3 minutes per side. Transfer the pineapple to a plate to cool.

Discard the oil used for the pineapple and wipe the pan clean. Add the remaining 3 tablespoons neutral oil to the pan and warm over medium-high heat. Once the oil just begins to smoke, reduce the heat to medium. Add 1 tortilla to the pan and cook until golden on both sides, about 20 seconds per side. Using tongs, transfer the crisped tortilla to a plate lined with paper towels. Repeat with the remaining 3 tortillas. Remove the pan from the heat, discard the oil, and wipe the pan clean again.

Add the black beans to the pan and place over medium heat. Mash three-quarters of the beans with the back of a fork. When the beans are hot, you should have something that looks similar to refried beans but a little chunkier. Season with a pinch of salt and remove from the heat.

In a large bowl, combine the onion, jalapeño, and drained octopus. Season with a pinch of salt and give a quick toss. Season generously with lime juice. Start with half a lime and work your way up from there if need be.

Using a cookie cutter, spoon, or small knife, cut out the core of your pineapple rings and slice them into ¼-inch (5 mm) batons. Naturally, some of the batons will be longer than others, and that's okay.

To assemble the tostadas, lay the fried tortillas out side by side. Divide the black beans among them and spread them over the tortillas, leaving about a 1-inch (2.5 cm) empty border around the edges. Dividing them evenly, lay the pineapple batons over the beans. Give the octopus mixture another quick toss. Reserving any liquid left in the bowl, pile the octopus mixture on top of the pineapple, giving each pile a gentle push so that it flattens out slightly. Top the octopus with the slices of avocado. Season the avocado lightly with salt. Drizzle any liquid remaining in the bowl over the tostadas. Garnish each tostada with the cilantro and serve immediately!

BARBECUED PINTO BEANS
WITH CHARRED OCTOPUS

Barbecued beans are a delicious addition to any cookout but take a few hours to cook. You can circumvent the long cooking process by adding your favorite smoky barbecue sauce to the beans. You'll want to make sure to use a nonstick pan (or, better yet, a well-seasoned cast-iron pan) to char the octopus. No sticking, beautiful color, and high heat are what you should aim for when cooking octopus.

SERVES 2

BARBECUED PINTO BEANS

2 tablespoons olive oil

4 cloves garlic, thinly sliced

½ cup (70 g) finely diced yellow onion

2 tablespoons minced jalapeño

1 teaspoon dried oregano

1 teaspoon Worcestershire sauce

½ cup (150 g) barbecue sauce, such as Sweet Baby Ray's Original

1 cup (225 g) dried pinto beans, soaked in water overnight

Kosher salt

CHARRED OCTOPUS SALAD

½ cup (40 g) thinly sliced red onion, shaved on a mandoline

2 tablespoons torn fresh mint

4 teaspoons fresh orange juice

2 teaspoons apple cider vinegar

1 tablespoon olive oil

Two 4-ounce (115 g) tins octopus in olive oil, drained

Kosher salt

To make the barbecued pinto beans: In a medium saucepan, combine the olive oil and garlic and cook over medium heat until the garlic becomes fragrant, a minute or two. Add the onion and cook until soft, about 4 minutes. Add the jalapeño and cook for another minute. Stir in the oregano, Worcestershire sauce, and barbecue sauce and remove from the heat.

Drain the beans of their soaking liquid and run cold water over them for a minute or so. (This helps to make the beans more digestible.) Add the rinsed beans to the pan with the barbecue sauce mix and pour in enough cold water to cover by about 1½ inches (4 cm). Bring the beans to a simmer over high heat. Then reduce to a slow simmer and cook until the beans are tender, about 1 hour. As the beans cook, the barbecue sauce will start to caramelize and stick to the sides of the pan, so scrape the sides of the pan every 10 minutes or so to get the sauce back into the beans. Season with salt. You want the beans to be creamy and not too wet. If the beans have a bit of liquid left, continue cooking them over medium heat until the sauce has reduced a bit.

To prepare the charred octopus salad: In a medium bowl, combine the onion, mint, orange juice, and vinegar.

Heat a cast-iron or nonstick pan over medium-high heat. Add the olive oil to the pan and when it just starts to smoke, add the octopus. Let the octopus rest, undisturbed, in the pan for 45 seconds before you give the pan a shake. Cook for another 30 seconds.

Remove the octopus from the pan with a slotted spoon, add it to the bowl with the onion mixture, and stir to incorporate. Season with salt.

Divide the barbecued beans between two bowls, top with even portions of the octopus salad, and pour any liquid left in the mixing bowl over the salad.

TROUT AND COD

SALMONIDAE AND GADIDAE

IN THE WORLD OF TINNED SEAFOOD, THERE AREN'T TOO MANY options when it comes to large-fin fish. Sure, you can find tinned tuna and salmon, but those tinned fish are two that should be avoided for sustainability reasons (with a few exceptions; Patagonia Provisions offers a lightly smoked sockeye salmon that is both sustainable and tasty). To fill this void, try tinned trout and cod.

Tinned trout is a great option if you're looking for a fish that is sustainable and healthful. Most trout sold commercially in the United States is farmed, with a large majority of that coming from Idaho. Trout is rated as a "best choice" by SeafoodWatch.org; it is low in fat, high in protein, and an excellent source of many nutrients the body needs, such as omega-3s, B vitamins, and potassium. These vitamins and minerals have many benefits, including reducing the risk of heart disease, promoting healthy bones and teeth, and building the immune system. In addition, trout is very low in mercury, which makes it an excellent option for a woman with a baby on the way.

Finding a good tinned cod is a bit trickier than finding good tinned trout because the cod population in the Atlantic Ocean has been overfished. You should look for cod from Alaska, Finland, Norway, or Iceland that has been caught with sustainable methods. The cod populations in these areas are protected, and the supply is growing. Cod is one of the most widely consumed fish in the world, and for good reason. Its sweet and flaky meat makes it enjoyable for any diner no matter how unadventurous. Cod is a very lean protein that is also low in calories and carbohydrates. It is high in B vitamins, which help metabolize nutrients in the body. It is also a good source of selenium, a mineral that helps make and protect your DNA. In addition, the nutrients and minerals found in cod help lower cholesterol and support brain function.

The recipes in this chapter will teach you to prepare such classic and familiar recipes as chowder and pasta with fish, olives, and tomatoes, but also light salads and accommodating scrambles.

WHAT'S IN THE TIN

Tinned trout comes primarily lightly smoked and stored in olive oil. It also comes in a pickled sauce or escabeche (see page 92). Tinned trout comes both skin-on and skinless. The skin is completely edible. Trout have small bones called pin bones that run down the center of the fillets after they have been removed from the spine. During the canning process, the bones become soft, almost nonexistent. They are edible, and just like the bones in tinned sardines, they are a great source of calcium. For the recipes in this book, look for trout that has been smoked and packed in olive oil. Skin off or on? It's up to you.

Tinned cod comes in several different flavors or sauces. Some of the more common tins are salt cod and cod with olive oil, tomato sauce, and Biscayne sauce (the famous Basque pepper sauce). Each recipe in this chapter calls for a specific type of tinned cod. The fillets are tinned boneless and sometimes with skin on. Skin-on or skin-off doesn't matter; use whichever one you have for these recipes.

SMOKED TROUT WITH GRAPEFRUIT AND AVOCADO

A simple lemon vinaigrette is all that's needed to dress this salad. Smoky tinned trout, acidic but still slightly sweet grapefruit, and rich mashed avocado are the perfect counterpoint to the assertive radicchio. Any radicchio will work here, but a heartier variety like Trevisano will hold up best.

MAKES 1 LARGE SALAD

1 avocado, halved and pitted

2 tablespoons olive oil

Lemon, for squeezing

Kosher salt

½ jalapeño, sliced into thin rings

¼ cup (20 g) thinly sliced red onion

¼ cup (35 g) roasted Marcona almonds, split in half

2 cups (100 g) shredded radicchio, cut to a ½-inch (1.5 cm) thickness

One 3.2-ounce (90 g) tin smoked trout in oil, oil reserved

1 grapefruit, segmented

Scoop the avocado flesh into a small bowl. Add 1 tablespoon of the olive oil and a squeeze of lemon juice. Mash with a fork until smooth and season with salt. Set aside.

In a large bowl, combine the jalapeño, onion, almonds, radicchio, and a pinch of salt and toss together. Add half of the oil from the trout tin, the trout, the remaining 1 tablespoon olive oil, and a squeeze of lemon juice. Toss together.

Pull a large serving bowl from the cupboard (or two if you'd like to serve smaller portions). Place the mashed avocado in the center of the bowl and spread it out a bit. Top the avocado with the grapefruit segments. Place the radicchio-trout mixture on top of the grapefruit segments. Enjoy!

SMOKED TROUT, SLAB BACON, AND TOMATO SALAD

The inspiration for this recipe comes from a famous steak house in Brooklyn, New York, that serves slabs of bacon alongside slices of raw tomato. Instead of raw beefsteak tomatoes, though, here you'll char up a handful of cherry tomatoes and make a quick dressing out of them. The smoked trout plays to the smokiness of the bacon and gives the dish a nice texture. Serve with a piece of crusty bread.

SERVES 2

2 thick slices slab bacon (4.8 ounces/135 g total)

1 tablespoon olive oil

1 cup (145 g) cherry tomatoes

¼ cup (20 g) thin half-moon slices red onion

8 thin slices jalapeño

2 teaspoons red wine vinegar

Kosher salt and freshly ground black pepper

One 3.2-ounce (90 g) tin smoked trout, drained

Crusty bread, for serving

Heat a skillet over medium-high heat until hot. Add the bacon slices and cook until beautifully golden on both sides, about 2 minutes per side. Transfer the bacon to a large bowl, but make sure to leave the fat behind in the pan.

Add the olive oil to the pan with the rendered bacon fat and return to medium-high heat. Add the tomatoes and cook until they are blistered with a bit of color, about 2 minutes. Swirl the pan a few times so that several sides of the tomatoes see the bottom of the pan. Remove from the heat and scrape everything from the pan into the bowl with the bacon using a silicone spatula. Be sure to scrape in all the fat; fat is your friend here.

Add the onion, jalapeño, and vinegar to the bowl. Using a fork or your hands, gently mash the tomatoes and toss everything together. Taste and season with salt. Taste again and season liberally with pepper.

Place a slice of bacon on each of two plates. Pull the smoked trout from the tin (skin on or off is up to you) and break it into large chunks over the bacon slices. Divide the onion and jalapeño slices evenly over the trout. Give the remaining juices in the bowl a few last stirs and spoon them over each plate. Enjoy the salad with a piece of crusty bread.

SMOKED TROUT CHOWDER

Homemade chowder is hearty enough for a cold, rainy-day meal but is deceptively light enough for a summertime meal as well. Tinned smoked trout comes with plenty of flavor, so you'll want to add it just before you plan on plating the chowder. This will help keep the flavors balanced. Also, to keep the dish meat-free, you can use vegetable stock instead of chicken stock.

SERVES 2

2 tablespoons unsalted butter

3 cloves garlic, minced

¼ cup (35 g) minced Spanish onion

¾ cup (110 g) fresh corn kernels

¼ cup (60 ml) white wine

1 cup (240 ml) chicken stock

½ cup (120 ml) whole milk

Leaves from 4 sprigs thyme

1 cup (140 g) red potato cubes (½ inch/ 1.5 cm)

½ cup (120 ml) heavy cream

1 scallion, thinly sliced

One 3.2-ounce (90 g) tin smoked trout

Kosher salt and freshly ground black pepper

Dill fronds, for garnish

In a medium saucepot, combine the butter and garlic and cook over medium-low heat until the garlic is fragrant, about 2 minutes. Add the onion and continue cooking until the onion is soft, about 5 minutes. Add the corn and cook for 1 minute.

Increase the heat to medium-high, add the wine, and let it reduce by half, 1 to 2 minutes. Add the stock and milk and bring to a simmer. Add the thyme leaves and potatoes, reduce to a gentle simmer, and cook until the potatoes are soft but not falling apart and the stock and milk have reduced by one-quarter or so, about 15 minutes.

Add the cream, scallion, and smoked trout. Bring the chowder back to a simmer and remove from the heat. Season with salt and pepper.

Spoon the chowder evenly into two bowls and garnish with a few dill fronds and a crack or two of black pepper.

SMOKED TROUT AND SCRAMBLED EGGS ON AN EVERYTHING BAGEL WITH HORSERADISH

The key to making this open-faced sandwich even better is to use high-quality trout, a good bagel, and plenty of fresh horseradish. Be sure to follow the directions below when it comes to layering the ingredients on the bagels. The order is intentional and will ensure that you are able to taste each ingredient on its own before ending with a delicious and harmonious bite.

MAKES 2 OPEN-FACED HALVES

1 everything bagel, halved horizontally

3 teaspoons unsalted butter

2 large eggs, whisked

Kosher salt and freshly ground black pepper

One 3.2-ounce (90 g) tin smoked trout in olive oil

Pinch of chili flakes, or more to taste

¼ cup (30 g) radish matchsticks

Small handful of dill fronds, picked

Lemon, for squeezing

Olive oil, for drizzling

½-inch (1.5 cm) piece fresh horseradish, peeled

Toast the bagel in a toaster or under the broiler. Immediately smear each half with 1 teaspoon of the butter.

In a nonstick skillet, heat the remaining 1 teaspoon butter over medium heat. When the butter has melted, add the eggs and constantly stir with a silicone spatula until they are cooked to the consistency that you prefer. To get eggs that are somewhat runny and hard, cook for about 2 minutes. Season the eggs with salt and pepper.

The way you build the bagel from here is important. You want the ingredients to remain on the bagel as you eat it. Dividing all the ingredients equally, build the sandwiches as instructed opposite.

Spoon the eggs onto the bagel halves. Remove the trout from the olive oil in the tin and flake the trout over the eggs. Add the chili flakes to the trout. Add, in this order, the radishes, a generous layer of dill, a squeeze of lemon juice, and a drizzle of olive oil. Using a Microplane, grate the horseradish on top of the dill. (Be as gentle as possible here. Too much pressure on the horseradish and you'll end up with a wet mess.) Add one or two cracks of black pepper over the top and enjoy.

SMOKED TROUT, GREEN BEANS, POTATOES, AND BASIL PESTO

Smoked trout with green beans and potatoes can be eaten hot, cold, as a plated dish, or tossed together as a salad. This recipe suggests serving it cold. Shocking blanched green vegetables in an ice bath ensures that they remain bright green; it also allows you to stop the cooking process immediately. For the warm version, time the cooking of your potatoes and green beans so they are done at the same time. Forgo allowing the potatoes to cool or shocking the beans and continue with the rest of the recipe.

SERVES 2

½ cup (15 g) fresh basil, roughly chopped

2 tablespoons pistachios

1 clove garlic, minced

2 tablespoons grated Parmesan cheese

¼ cup (60 ml) olive oil

1 teaspoon red wine vinegar

Kosher salt

9 ounces (255 g) peewee potatoes

3 ounces (85 g) green beans, trimmed

Two 3.2-ounce (90 g) tins smoked trout, drained

Lemon, for squeezing

In a food processor, combine the basil, pistachios, garlic, and Parmesan and pulse a few times. With the machine running, slowly drizzle in the olive oil. Pour the vinegar into the basil mixture and pulse a few times (see Note). Season with salt. What you are looking for is a pesto that has some texture but isn't overly chunky. The pieces of pistachio will add a pleasant crunch to the potatoes.

In a small pot, combine the potatoes and cold water to cover by 2 inches (5 cm). Season liberally with salt. Bring to a simmer over high heat, then immediately turn down to a gentle simmer and cook until you can easily pierce a potato with a knife or fork, about 10 minutes. Remove the potatoes from the water with a slotted spoon and transfer to a plate to cool.

Meanwhile, make an ice bath. Place enough ice and cold water in a large bowl to cover the green beans two times over. Fill a medium pot with water and bring to a boil over high heat. Season liberally with salt. Carefully place the beans in the boiling water and cook until just tender, 2 or 3 minutes. Transfer the beans to the ice bath using a slotted spoon or skimmer. When the beans have cooled completely, remove them from the water and place them on a kitchen towel to dry.

To serve, transfer the trout to two plates. Squeeze a little lemon juice over the green beans and divide them between the plates. Place the potatoes in the bowl with the pesto and toss to coat. Place the potatoes on the plates alongside the trout and beans.

NOTE: If you are making the pesto ahead of time, do not add the vinegar and transfer the pesto to an airtight container. The reason you don't add the vinegar until you are ready to use the pesto is because the acid starts turning the color of the pesto less vibrant as soon as it's added.

TINNED COD
BRANDADE

Brandade is a classic dish from Provence, France, but it is eaten in most Mediterranean countries. When you make the dish using tinned salt cod, the recipe is a snap—there's no need to soak the salt cod in water for 24 hours before proceeding. The addition of the potatoes helps mellow the salt cod's intensity, making this version a good choice for first-time eaters of brandade. This dish is made to eat on toast slices, but it's also especially good next to an arugula salad dressed with only a bit of olive oil and lemon juice.

SERVES 2

7 ounces (200 g) Yukon Gold potatoes, peeled but left whole

3 bay leaves

2 cloves garlic, smashed

Kosher salt

3 tablespoons heavy cream

¼ cup (60 ml) olive oil, plus more for finishing

One 4.4-ounce (125 g) tin salt cod in olive oil, oil reserved

1 baguette, warmed in the oven and sliced ½ inch (1.5 cm) thick

In a small pot, combine the potatoes, bay leaves, garlic, and enough cold water to cover by 2 inches (5 cm). Season with salt to the point where you can just taste the salt. You always want to start potatoes in cold water when cooking them this way. This will ensure that your potatoes cook evenly. No one likes a potato that's crunchy on the inside and mushy on the outside. You'll know the potatoes are cooked when you can slide a sharp knife into the center of the potato with a little resistance but it slides out easily. Bring to a boil over high heat. Immediately turn down to a gentle simmer and cook until the potatoes are cooked through, about 20 minutes.

With a slotted spoon, transfer the potatoes and garlic to a food processor. Discard the bay leaves but reserve the cooking liquid.

Pulse the potatoes three or four times to break them up. Add the cream and pulse three more times. With the machine running, slowly drizzle in the olive oil followed by the reserved oil from the tin. Add the cod and blend until smooth. The mixture should have the consistency of slightly thick mashed potatoes. If your brandade is a bit too thick, add the reserved cooking liquid 1 tablespoon at a time to reach the desired consistency. Taste and season with salt.

Transfer the brandade to a serving bowl and drizzle with a bit more olive oil. Serve with warm baguette slices alongside.

LINGUINE WITH COD, TOMATOES, AND BLACK OLIVES

Linguine with cod is a great pasta for when you are short on time but need something satisfying. You can make it with pantry ingredients, but the better the ingredients, especially the canned tomatoes, the better your result will be. When hand-crushing the tomatoes, be sure to use a deep bowl and make a small hole in the tomato with your thumb before fully crushing it. Otherwise, you may end up with tomato juice on your shirt.

SERVES 2

3 tablespoons olive oil

4 cloves garlic, smashed

2 tablespoons minced shallot

½ teaspoon chili flakes

5 canned whole peeled tomatoes, hand-crushed

⅓ cup (50 g) cured black olives

Kosher salt

6 ounces (170 g) linguine or any pasta shape you have

One 4.2-ounce (120 g) tin cod in olive oil

⅓ cup (10 g) fresh basil, torn

Bring a large pot of water to a boil over high heat for the pasta. This can take up to 20 minutes, depending on your stove. Use this time to gather the rest of your ingredients.

In a skillet, heat the olive oil and garlic over medium heat and cook until both sides of the garlic cloves are golden and the smell of garlic permeates your kitchen, about 1 minute per side. Add the shallot and cook until it becomes translucent and soft, about 2 minutes.

Remove the pan from the heat and add the chili flakes. Let the pan rest for a minute or two before adding the crushed tomatoes and olives. so that the tomatoes won't start splattering the second they hit the hot pan.

Add enough salt to the boiling water so that it reminds you of a less salty sea. Add the pasta and cook according to the package directions, stirring the pasta every 2 minutes or so to ensure that it doesn't stick together. Taste a noodle a minute or so before the end of the suggested cooking time to ensure that your pasta comes out al dente.

Continued

Return the pan to medium-high heat. Reserving ⅓ cup (80 ml) of the pasta cooking water, drain the pasta and add to the pan along with the reserved pasta water. Stir and flip the pasta in the sauce until the sauce has reduced by half, about 1 minute.

Reserving the oil in the tin, place the cod in the pan with the pasta. Using your spoon, spatula, or tongs, gently break the cod into smaller pieces. Remove the pan from the heat and add the torn basil. Slowly add the oil from the tin into the pasta while stirring.

Divide the pasta between two bowls and serve.

COD IN BISCAYNE SAUCE WITH CHARD AND SAFFRON RICE

Biscayne sauce is a traditional sauce found in the Basque region of Spain. It is made with the choricero pepper (or ñora chile), which is more commonly seen in the form of sweet paprika in the United States. In this dish, the cod in Biscayne sauce is served over a bowl of saffron rice. Saffron is expensive and best when it is fresh, so you'll want to refrain from using the stuff you bought a year ago that has been hiding in the back of your spice rack. Most reputable spice shops (see Resources, page 196) sell saffron in very small quantities so you can buy just what you need.

SERVES 2

Small pinch of saffron

1 cup (240 ml) boiling water

¼ cup (35 g) finely diced yellow onion

3 tablespoons olive oil

½ cup (100 g) jasmine or other long-grain rice

Kosher salt

2 cloves garlic, thinly sliced

4 cups (120 g) packed Swiss chard leaves, torn into pieces the size of playing cards

Two 4-ounce (111 g) tins cod in Biscayne sauce (see Note)

1 tablespoon unsalted butter

Place the saffron in a small heatproof bowl. Pour the boiling water over the saffron to bloom. (Blooming the saffron just means that you are applying heat to extract as much of the flavor and aroma as possible.) Set aside.

In a small saucepot, combine the onion and 1 tablespoon of the olive oil and cook over medium heat until the onion is soft but shows no color, about 3 minutes. Add the rice and stir a few times so that the onion and rice meld together.

Pour the saffron water over the rice, add a pinch of salt, and give a quick stir. Increase the heat to medium-high and cook until the rice comes to a boil. Immediately reduce the heat to low, cover, and cook, undisturbed, until the rice is tender and the water is absorbed, about 20 minutes. Remove from the heat and crack the lid.

Continued

In a skillet, combine the remaining 2 tablespoons olive oil and the garlic and toast the garlic over medium-high heat for only a minute or two. Add the Swiss chard and toss and stir with a wooden spoon or silicone spatula, scraping the bottom of the pan so that the garlic mixes with the greens and doesn't burn. (If the garlic gets too dark, you'll want to start over with clean oil and fresh garlic. When garlic burns, it gets very bitter and is super unpleasant.) Cook until the chard is wilted but still has a bit of texture, about 2 minutes. Season with a pinch of salt. Remove from the heat.

Uncover the pot of rice and fluff the rice with a fork. Divide the rice between two bowls. Top with the Swiss chard.

Wipe the pan clean. Open both tins of cod and pour them into the pan. Try to keep the cod fillets whole and get every last bit of sauce out of the tins and into the pan. Add a small splash of water and set the pan over medium heat. Add the butter and swirl the pan a few times to emulsify the sauce. Using a spoon, baste the cod fillets with the Biscayne sauce to coat the cod and help heat the fish through. This process will take only 2 minutes or so.

Immediately divide the fillets between the bowls and spoon the sauce over the entire dish.

Gozoak!

NOTE: For the cod in Biscayne sauce, seek out Donostia Foods brand (see Resources, page 196).

DONOSTIA
F O O D S
selected ingredients for authentic pintxos and tapas

Cod Fish
in Biscayne sauce

Bacalao a la Vizcaína
con
Aceite de Oliva

NET WEIGHT 4 oz (111 g)

cole's
trout

smoked trout

with lemon & cracked pepper

SUSTAINABLE
SELECTIONS

bpa-free – no preservatives
Net Wt 3.2 oz (91g)

SCOUT

ONTARIO TROUT
WITH DILL

TRUITE DE L'ONTARIO
ET ANETH

PRODUCT OF
CANADA

PRODUIT DU
CANADA

NET WT. 3.1 OZ | 90G

RESOURCES

Nowadays you can shop for anything online, and tinned fish is no different. That said, I encourage you to find a mom-and-pop shop before giving way to the ease of ordering online. You never know what else you'll find when you shop in person. If you must order online, here are some of my favorite resources for tinned fish and other helpful ingredients.

ANSON MILLS
803-467-4122
ANSONMILLS.COM
Heirloom flour and grains

BUON'ITALIA
212-633-9090
BUONITALIA.COM
Anchovies, pasta, and olive oils

CAPUTO'S MARKET AND DELI
801-531-8669
CAPUTOS.COM
Tinned fish and pasta

DESPAÑA
212-219-5050
DESPANABRANDFOODS.COM
Tinned fish and chorizo

DONOSTIA FOODS
312-997-5181
DONOSTIAFOODS.COM
Tinned fish and saffron

LA TIENDA
800-710-4304
TIENDA.COM
Tinned fish and chorizo

MURRAY'S CHEESE
888-692-4339
MURRAYSCHEESE.COM
Tinned fish, cheese, crackers, and 'nduja

RANCHO GORDO
707-529-1935
RANCHOGORDO.COM
Dried heirloom beans

SOS CHEFS
212-505-5813
SOS.CHEFS.COM
Spices, grains, and dried beans

WHITE OAK PASTURES
229-641-2081
WHITEOAKPASTURES.COM
Grass-fed and pastured beef, lamb,
and pork

YUMMY BAZAAR
844-986-6922
YUMMYBAZAAR.COM
Tinned fish

ZINGERMAN'S DELICATESSEN
312-997-5181
ZINGERMANSDELI.COM
Tinned fish, bacon, and 'nduja

ACKNOWLEDGMENTS

Thank you:

To my lovely wife, Natalie, for believing in me even when I don't, and for lovingly allowing me to always be myself. For pushing me to be better every day. For being the peanut butter to my mayonnaise in the adventure of parenting. Being married to a chef isn't easy, but you unselfishly let me share our love with the kitchen. I don't want to do anything without you.

To my son, Gus. You are the best thing I've ever done. You brighten my life in ways I didn't know were possible. You are a constant motivation to be a better father, husband, cook, and man. You are crazy, independent, and boisterous. Please never change. I love you.

To my agent, David Black, for helping make this book a reality. Not only do you support me at my restaurant, but you also assisted in rounding out the idea of the book. Your love of tinned fish and your unrelenting appetite for life are inspiring.

To Judy Pray, Lia Ronnen, and the entire Artisan team for answering all of my questions, providing veracious guidance, and giving this book a voice. Judy, thank you for taking a chance and turning an idea into reality. Sibylle Kazeroid, Kate Slate, Zachary R. Townsend, Nina Simoneaux, Nancy Murray, and Erica Huang, thank you for your hard work making me look good on these pages. Thank you to Raphael Geroni for the beautiful book design.

Continued

To Dana Gallagher, Frances Boswell, and Ali Elly, thank you for bringing the recipes in this book to life with beautiful photographs and artwork. Tinned fish has never looked so good.

A special thanks to Nicole Krasinski, Stuart Brioza, and Tom Colicchio for reading this book and giving me your stamps of approval. It's chefs like you who are anchors while still pushing the boundaries of what is good about our industry; you are an endless source of inspiration.

This book was born in the NICU alongside my son. My wife and I will always send all of our love to the nurses and doctors who made sure our son came home; they're Gus's angels.

INDEX

Note: Page numbers in italics refer to illustrations.

CHRIS MCDADE is the chef and owner of Popina, an Italian restaurant with Southern touches, located in Brooklyn, New York. Previously he was a chef with the Union Square Hospitality Group's Maialino and Marta and worked in the kitchens of Cafe Altro Paradiso and KR Steak Bar, among others. He lives in Brooklyn with his wife and son. Follow him on Instagram at @alwaysanchovy.